Eve's Revenge

ALSO BY TAMA STARR

The "Natural Inferiority" of Women:
Outrageous Pronouncements by Misguided Males

TAMA STARR

Eve's Revenge

SAINTS, SINNERS, AND STAND-UP

SISTERS ON THE ULTIMATE

EXTINCTION OF MEN

HARCOURT BRACE & COMPANY

New York   San Diego   London

Requests for permission to make copies of any part of the work
should be mailed to: Permissions, Harcourt Brace & Company,
6277 Sea Harbor Drive, Orlando, Florida 32887-6777.

Text credits appear on page 264.

Library of Congress Cataloging-in-Publication Data
Eve's revenge: saints, sinners, and stand-up sisters on the ultimate
extinction of men/compiled by Tama Starr.—1st ed.
p.   cm.
Includes index.
ISBN 0-15-100084-0
1. Men—Quotations, maxims, etc.   2. Men—Humor.   3. Sex—
Quotations, maxims, etc.   4. Sex—Humor.   I. Starr, Tama.
PN6084.M4E94   1994
808.88'2—dc20   94-4497

Designed by Lisa Peters
Illustration research by Roberta Rosenthal,
RSR Designs, New York
Cover illustration: Collage © 1994
by Tama Starr and Roberta Rosenthal
Printed in the United States of America
First edition
A B C D E

To my mother,

Jean Melman Starr

CONTENTS

Contents

Nobody will ever win the battle of the sexes.
There's too much fraternizing with the enemy.

—*Henry Kissinger*

Men Once Roamed the Earth

❧ DID YOU KNOW *the earth was once infested with creatures called "men"? Wherever you went you were likely to see them. No place was safe. As recently as our grandmothers' time they ran wild everywhere, promoting their filthy habits, their bottomless needs, their merciless violence.*

Thank Goddess, that is no longer the case. The Great Millennial Revolution eliminated the masculine culture of competition and strife and inaugurated the longest reign of peace the world has seen since "men" first invented war. Now that "men" have gone the way of the dodo and the pterodactyl, and the One World Govern(person)t of Cooperation rules, war will never reign again!

We have all seen videos of the pleasant encamp(person)ts where the remaining breeding speci(person)s follow their traditional manly pursuits: drumming, producing arts and crafts (the sale of which helps finance the camps) and printing money. What is money? you ask. Money was an excrescence employed by "men" to measure worth. Today, like "men," it exists only as a relic. In the pre-Revolutionary era "making money" and "waging war" were the quintessential male occupations, and today we deem it wise to allow the speci(person)s to continue to enjoy at least one of these activities lest they yearn after the other. "Men" do possess a rudi(person)tary intelligence, and deprived of amuse(person)t they tend to languish.

∽ Despite the success of the camp system, however, the inconvenience and expense of breeding these unnatural beings and then maintaining them in the unearned luxury they enjoy render the continuance of the program problematic.

Im(person)se credit is due to those sapients who toil in the laboratories where the creatures are (person)ufactured and who, overcoming natural repugnance, nurture them up to the age of one week, when they are turned over to their own. The speci(person)s display an almost sapient affection for their young, feeding them the best morsels and educating them in their manly traditions. Severe punish(person)ts were necessary in the early days to counteract the perpetuation among them of such pernicious habits as writing and reading, which led inevitably to their building communications devices. Today such practices have largely died out among them, and such discipline is no longer necessary.

Camp (person)age(person)t is nonetheless extraordinarily difficult. It is impossible adequately to reward those sapients who selflessly undertake it. Some of the horrors they are forced to witness are indescribable. The merest view of a sapient drives the beasts to frenzies. Given their rudi(person)tary verbal skills, the creatures are more disgusting than the masturbating monkeys at Khajuraho.

Keeping the speci(person)s separated from one another presents additional challenges. It is necessary to restrict their association to gatherings of less than five: in larger numbers they display an antisocial inclination to group themselves into "teams" and play competitive sports, the dreadful consequences of which need not be delineated here.

All in all, the surviving "men" have adapted so well to their luxurious accommodations that the excess of the male survival instinct over its actual equip(person)t for survival is a pheno(person)on perhaps worth studying before the entire experi(person)t is phased out.

It is the inefficiency, danger and sheer uselessness of the male preservation program that causes (person)y sapients to question its worth. There is always the dreaded (person)ace that some of them might escape, frustrating the destiny Goddess has decreed for them. As She knows, there is no conceivable positive contribution they can make to our now-perfect society. Science has eliminated "men" for breeding: anyone can clone herself and birth a daughter; lovers can combine their XX chromosomes and birth daughters who possess the goddesslike characteristics of both of them. "Men," in fact, are required only for the purpose of breeding more "men."

Why, then, do we continue to maintain these mutants?

Three factors have contributed to their survival: the historic compassion of sapients (formerly known as "women"); the interests of scientific investigation (how do their brains work? We still don't know); and the senti(person)al tenets of environ(person)talism, which hold every species, however useless, worthy to endure. We may assume that in future a more rigorous cost-benefit analysis will prevail, and "men"'s behavior will be consigned to textbooks, their crippled Y chromosomes to the spore labs, and "men" themselves to herstory.

Naturally, we will continue to mother them for as long as absolutely necessary.

✎ *Now let us celebrate the philosophers who gestated and bore the Great Millennial Revolution. Who were these geniae?*

Too (person)y of the greatest, sadly, remain unknown. "Men" in their day exercised iron control over all speech and media, so sapient culture was largely oral. We will commemorate the anonymous jests sapients once employed to lighten their subjugation, and we will also pay (fem)age to all mothers through the ages who whispered to daughters the secrets of controlling "men," so that despite universal and total oppression, wo(person) (person)aged to survive.

We will also laud the great sapient philosophers—Marilyn Monroe and St. Theresa, Roseanne Arnold and Mary Wollstonecraft, Zsa Zsa Gabor and Marie de Sévigné, and numerous others—who courageously exploited their eminence in the heteropatriarchal establish(person)t to further the Fem Supreme Revolution. The prolific Anon. and influential collectives such as Women Against Sex will not be forgotten. The thoughts of some "men" are included as well: those who, in the immortal words of the great Valerie Solanis, "cooperated in their own destruction and rode the waves to their demise."

✎ *This book portrays the world as it was at the end of the era when "men" still stalked the earth. It is the textbook of the Fem Supreme Revolution: a compendium of the universe-shattering philosophy that birthed the compassionate and eternal world we know today. Examples from three millennia of Femthought have been so simply and authentically assembled that even "men," if they still knew how to read, could understand it.*

From definitions of those creatures known as "men," through time-honored strategies for domesticating them and a discussion of what used to be known as Sex, to the revolutionary theories underlying the ultimate fe(person) triumph, students and scholars will delight in uncovering the true herstory of Eve's conquest of Man the Beast.

— Tama Starr, a Sapient ("One Who Knows")
(Person)hattan, New York: Autumn, 2094

Know the Enemy

To understand those strange creatures called "men," let us begin with some definitions by a bevy of sadder-but-wiser experts.

WHAT IS MAN?

Men are nicotine-soaked, beer-besmirched, whiskey-greased, red-eyed devils!
— CARRY NATION (1846–1911)

Men are the devil—they all bring woe.
In winter it's easy to say just "No."
Men are the devil, that's one sure thing.
But what are you going to do in the spring?

— MARY CAROLYN DAVIES,
"A Prayer for Every Day," c. 1925

Man is merely dust, and woman settles him.　　　— ANON.

What is man, when you come to think upon him, but a minutely set, ingenious machine for turning, with infinite artfulness, the red wine of Shiraz into urine?
— ISAK DINESEN, "The Dreamers," 1934

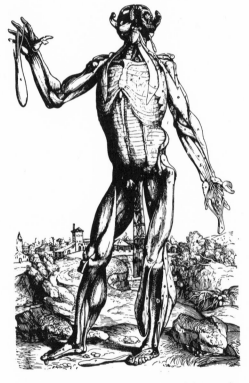

THE MALE ANIMAL

∾· *The overwhelming consensus, however, was that men are neither as simple as dust nor as complex as machines, but, rather, more accurately described as . . .*

. . . beasts, and even beasts don't behave as they do.
— BRIGITTE BARDOT

. . . those creatures with two legs and eight hands.
— JAYNE MANSFIELD (1932–1967)

. . . unusually low voices; short life expectancies; odd, drab costumes; a tendency to sweat, fart and yell.　　— C. E. CRIMMINS

✑ *Man is . . .*

. . . a worm. He comes along, wriggles a bit, and then some chickens get him.

— ANON.

. . . a domestic animal which, if treated with firmness and kindness, can be trained to do most things.

— JILLY COOPER

✑ *Not everyone agrees that the male is trainable.*

A snake will always be a snake, even if you put a chain around its neck and try to make it walk upright.

— LISA ALTHER, *Kinflicks,* 1975

My first husband was such an animal that when he went to the zoo, he had to buy two tickets. One to get in and one to get out!

— UNKNOWN

[Sadie] gathered herself together. No one could describe the scorn of her expression or the contemptuous hatred she put into her answer.

"You men! You filthy dirty pigs! You're all the same, all of you. Pigs! Pigs!"

— W. SOMERSET MAUGHAM, *Rain,* 1923

> *Certain domestic animals were venerated above men—with good reason.*

The more I see of men the more I admire dogs.

— Marie de Sévigné (1626–1696)

Let us love dogs, let us only love dogs! Men and cats are unworthy creatures.

— Maria Konstantinova Bashkirtsev (1860–1884)

Some of my best leading men have been dogs and horses.

— Elizabeth Taylor

I never married because there was no need. I have three pets at home which answer the same purpose as a husband. I have a dog which growls every morning, a parrot which swears all afternoon and a cat that comes home late at night.

— Marie Corelli (1855–1924)

> *In all fairness . . .*

All men are not slimy warthogs. Some men are silly giraffes, some woebegone puppies, some insecure frogs. But if one is not careful, those slimy warthogs can ruin it for all the others.

— Cynthia Heimel

A man—despite some similarities—is not like dog droppings. For one thing, he's probably too big to just step over.

— Dorian Yeager

A rattlesnake that doesn't bite teaches you nothing.

— JESSAMYN WEST, *The Life I Really Lived,* 1979

⟶ Even men concurred on the essentially animal nature of the male beast.

Men, my dear, are very queer animals—a mixture of horse-nervousness, ass-stubbornness and camel-malice.

— THOMAS HENRY HUXLEY, letter to Mrs. W. K. Clifford, FEBRUARY 10, 1895

⟶ With the self-absorption characteristic of the species, "men" put prodigious effort into self-definition. While they may have believed they were including WOMEN *in their analysis of the* huMAN *condition, they clearly had only themselves in mind as they reiterated the pompous phrase (rarely used by sapients),* MAN IS . . .

. . . a civic animal.   — ARISTOTLE (384–322 B.C.)

. . . a social animal.   — SENECA (4 B.C.–A.D.64)

. . . a tool-making animal.   — BENJAMIN FRANKLIN, 1778

. . . a puny, slow, awkward, unarmed animal.

— JACOB BRONOWSKI, *The Ascent of Man,* 1974

. . . the only animal that plays poker.   — DON HEROLD

. . . the only animal that laughs and has a state legislature.

— SAMUEL BUTLER (1835–1902)

. . . an animal, and until his immediate material and economic needs are satisfied, he cannot develop further.

— W. H. AUDEN (1907–1973)

. . . a make-believe animal—he is never so truly himself as when he is acting a part. — WILLIAM HAZLITT (1778–1830)

. . . an animal . . . [whose] chief occupation is the extermination of other animals and his own species, which, however, multiplies with such insistent rapidity as to infest the whole habitable earth and Canada. — AMBROSE BIERCE, *The Devil's Dictionary,* 1906

...a rational animal who always loses his temper when he is called upon to act in accordance with the dictates of reason.

— OSCAR WILDE (1854–1900)

...the only animal that can remain on friendly terms with the victims he intends to eat until he eats them.　— SAMUEL BUTLER

...little inferior to the tiger and the hyena in cruelty and savagery.　— ARTHUR SCHOPENHAUER, *Parerga und Paralipomena,* 1851

...more an ape than many of the apes.

— FRIEDRICH NIETZSCHE, *Thus Spake Zarathustra,* 1891

...[one who] like an angry ape
plays such fantastick tricks before high heaven
as make the angels weep...

— WILLIAM SHAKESPEARE, *Measure for Measure,* 1604

...a toad-eating animal. The admiration of power in others is as common to men as the love of it in himself; the one makes him a tyrant, the other a slave.　— WILLIAM HAZLITT

...a noble animal, splendid in ashes, and pompous in the grave, solemnizing nativities and deaths with equal lustre, not omitting ceremonies of bravery, in the infamy of his nature.

— SIR THOMAS BROWNE (1605–1682)

...the most formidable of all beasts of prey, and, indeed, the only one that preys systematically on its own species.

— WILLIAM JAMES (1842–1910)

...a dog's ideal of what God should be. — HOLBROOK JACKSON

O man! thou feeble tenant of an hour,
Debased by slavery, or corrupt by power,
Who knows thee well must quit thee with disgust,
Degraded mass of animated dust!
Thy love is lust, thy friendship all a cheat,
Thy smiles hypocrisy, thy word deceit!
By nature vile, ennobled out by name,
Each kindred brute might bid thee blush for shame.
— LORD BYRON, "On the Monument of a Newfoundland Dog," 1808

Poor little men! Poor little strutting peacocks! They spread out their tails as conquerors almost as soon as they are able to walk.
— JEAN ANOUILH, *Cécile,* 1949

The bachelor is a peacock, the engaged man a lion, and the married man a jackass. — GERMAN PROVERB

🖎 *These primitive qualities begin to explain the mentality of "men."*

I have always thought that the difference between a man and a mule is that a mule could change his mind.
— ABIGAIL DUNIWAY, Oregon women's rights pioneer (1834–1915)

The only time a woman really succeeds in changing a man is when he's a baby.   — NATALIE WOOD (1938–1981)

Maleness is wonderful, really, isn't it, honey? Perfect denial of reality.   — ERICA JONG, *Any Woman's Blues*, 1990

MAN THE CHILD

🖎 *The worst-kept secret in the history of civilization:*

As long as you know that most men are like children, you know everything.
— COCO CHANEL (1883–1971)

I like men to behave like men—strong and childish.
— FRANÇOISE SAGAN

෨• *The childishness of men is not news—even to men.*

There's no such thing as a man ... just a little boy in a man's body.
— ELVIS PRESLEY (1935–1977), quoted in *Playboy,* MAY 1993

Dig it, this is a planet of women. . . . The men are just guests here. Women are the mothers, the ones who bear the life of new generations. It's like they have the greatest creative energy going for them. Women today are not satisfied. . . . They want men, but all they find are little boys. — CHARLES MANSON

Men are but children, though they have gray hairs; they are only of a larger size. — SENECA

Men come of age at sixty, women at fifteen.
— JAMES STEPHENS, in *The Observer* (London), OCTOBER 1, 1944

A bachelor never quite gets over the idea that he is a thing of beauty and a boy forever. — HELEN ROWLAND (1876–1950)

Men get opinions as boys learn to spell,
By reiteration chiefly.
— ELIZABETH BARRETT BROWNING (1806–1861)

෨• *An outstanding number of speci(person)s never even mature from infancy into childhood.*

A man's home may seem to be his castle on the outside; inside, it is more often his nursery. — CLARE BOOTHE LUCE (1903–1987)

I blame Rousseau, myself. "Man is born free," indeed. Man is not born free, he is born attached to his mother by a cord and is not capable of looking after himself for at least seven years (seventy in some cases).

— KATHARINE WHITEHORN, British columnist

Man is of Woman born and her face bends over him in infancy with an expression he can never quite forget.

— MARGARET FULLER, 1843

Much male fear of feminism is infantilism—the longing to remain the mother's son, to possess a woman who exists purely for him. These infantile needs of adult men for women have been sentimentalized and romanticized long enough as "love"; it is time to recognize them as arrested development. — ADRIENNE RICH

⟡ *A contrarian speaks out:*

I refuse to consign the whole male sex to the nursery. I insist on believing that some men are my equals. — BRIGID BROPHY

⟡ *If most "men" are arrested in babyhood, what must we conclude they love yummy-best in the whole big wide world?*

What men like is a woman with an oversized bust and an undersized brain.

— EVA GABOR, in the New York *Daily News,* DECEMBER 27, 1992

Q: A man is dating three women and wants to get married. He has to decide which one to ask. He gives them each $1,000. The first one spends $800 on clothes and puts the other $200 in the bank. The second one spends $200 on clothes and puts the other $800 in the bank. The third one puts the whole $1,000 in the bank. Which one does he marry?

A: The one with big breasts.

— U.S. JOKE, C. 1990

BEAUTY VS. BRAINS

∾ *It's no wonder that "men" always found pretty girls so much more* **interesting** *than intelligent women.*

It is better for a girl to have beauty than brains because boys see better than they think. — UNKNOWN

Beauty's the thing that counts
In women; red lips
And black eyes are better than brains.
— MARY CAROLYN DAVIES, "Beauty's the Thing," C. 1925

A real woman is a young, pretty, sexy, tender woman who is no taller than five feet six who adores you.
— FRANÇOISE PARTURIER, *Open Letter to Men,* 1968

'Tis hard we should be by the men despised,
Yet kept from knowing what would make us prized;
Debarred from knowledge, banished from the schools,
And with the utmost industry bred fools;
Laughed out of reason, jested out of sense,
And nothing left but native innocence,
Then told we are incapable of wit,
And only for the meanest drudgeries fit;
Made slaves to serve their luxury and pride,
And with innumerable hardships tried . . .
As if we were for nothing else designed,
But made, like puppets, to divert mankind.

— LADY MARY CHUDLEIGH, *The Ladies Defence,* 1701

∾ *A candid man:*

I like young girls. Their stories are shorter.   — TOM McGUANE

∾ *Secrets of glamour experts:*

Any girl can be glamorous; all you have to do is stand still and act stupid.   — HEDY LAMARR

It isn't that gentlemen really prefer blondes, it's just that we look dumber.   — ANITA LOOS (1894–1981)

Men are always ready to respect anything that bores them.

— MARILYN MONROE (1926–1962)

God made men stronger but not necessarily more intelligent. He gave women intuition and femininity. And, used properly, that combination easily jumbles the brain of any man I've ever met.
— FARRAH FAWCETT

Sex appeal is fifty percent what you've got and fifty percent what people think you've got.
— SOPHIA LOREN

Plain women know more about men than beautiful ones do.
— KATHARINE HEPBURN

❧ *Insights by intellectuals:*

In general all curvaceousness strikes men as incompatible with the life of the mind.
— FRANÇOISE PARTURIER, *Open Letter to Men,* 1968

Have they not prohibited us from cultivating an acquaintance with the sciences? Do they not regard the woman who suffers her faculties to rust in a state of listless indolence, with a more favourable eye, than her who engages in a dispassionate search after truth?
— MARY SCOTT, *The Female Advocate,* 1774

Men seldom make passes
At girls who wear glasses.
— DOROTHY PARKER, "News Item," *Enough Rope,* 1926

The usual masculine disillusionment is in discovering that a woman has a brain.

— Margaret Mitchell, *Gone with the Wind,* 1936

Man forgives woman anything save the wit to outwit him.

— Minna Antrim, *Naked Truth and Veiled Illusions,* 1902

'Tis thus ye rail to vent your spleen,
And think your wondrous wit is seen:
But 'tis the malice of your sex appears.
   What, suffer women to pretend to sense!
   Oh! how this optic magnifies the offense,
      And aggravates your fears!
   ... What is it from our sex ye fear,
      That thus ye curb our powers?
   D'ye apprehend a bookish war,
Or are your judgements less for raising ours?
   Come, come, the real truth confess
   (A fault acknowledged is the less),
   And own it was an avaricious soul
Which would, with greedy eyes, monopolise the whole;
   And bars us learning on the selfish score,
      That, conscious of our native worth,
      Ye dread to make it more.

— Elizabeth Thomas, from "On Sir J—— S—— saying in a
Sarcastic Manner, My Books would Make me Mad. An Ode," 1722

NATURAL-BORN FOOLS

>*Let us dispose once and for all of the vexed question of the comparative intelligence of the two sexes.*

A woman's appetite is twice that of a man's; her sexual desire, four times; her intelligence, eight times. — SANSKRIT PROVERB

I'm furious about the Women's Liberationists. They keep getting up on soapboxes and proclaiming that women are brighter than men. That's true, but it should be kept very quiet or it ruins the whole racket.

— ANITA LOOS, in *The Observer* (London), DECEMBER 30, 1973

>*H. L. Mencken on "the feminine mind":*

The Maternal Instinct

A man's women folk, whatever their outward show of respect for his merit and authority, always regard him secretly as an ass, and with something akin to pity. His most gaudy sayings and doings seldom deceive them; they see the actual man within, and know him for a shallow and pathetic fellow. In this fact, perhaps, lies one of the best proofs of feminine intelligence. . . .

This shrewd perception of masculine bombast and make-believe, this acute understanding of man as the eternal tragic comedian, is at the bottom of that compassionate irony which passes under the name of the maternal instinct. A woman wishes to mother a man simply because she sees into his helplessness, his need of an amiable environment, his touching self-delusion. . . .

Women's Intelligence

That it should still be necessary at this late stage in the senility of the human race to argue that women have a fine and fluent intelligence is surely an eloquent proof of the defective observation, incurable prejudice, and general imbecility of their lords and masters. . . .

Women, in truth, are not only intelligent; they have almost a monopoly of certain of the subtler and more utile forms of intelligence. . . . Find me an obviously intelligent man, a man free from sentimentality and illusion, a man hard to deceive, a man of the first class, and I'll show you a man with a wide streak of woman in him. . . . The caveman is all muscles and mush. Without a woman to rule him and think for him, he is a truly lamentable spectacle: a baby with whiskers, a rabbit with the frame of an aurochs, a feeble and preposterous caricature of God. . . .

The Masculine Bag of Tricks

What men, in their egoism, constantly mistake for a deficiency of intelligence in women is merely an incapacity for mastering that mass of small intellectual tricks . . . which constitutes the chief mental equipment of the average male. . . . One could not think of Aristotle or Beethoven multiplying 3,472,701 by 99,999 without making a mistake, nor could one think of him remembering the range of this or that railway share for two years, or the number of ten-penny nails in a hundredweight. . . . This lack of skill at manual and mental tricks of a trivial [kind] . . . is a character that men of the first class share with women of the first, second and even third classes. . . .

The Thing Called Intuition

Men, as every one knows, are disposed to question this superior intelligence of women. . . . But though every normal man thus cherishes the soothing unction that he is the intellectual superior of all women, and particularly of his wife, he constantly gives the lie to his pretension by consulting and deferring to what he calls her intuition. . . .

Intuition? With all respect, bosh! Then it was intuition that led Darwin to work out the hypothesis of natural selection. Then it was intuition that fabricated the gigantically complex score of "Die Walküre." Then it was intuition that convinced Columbus of the existence of land to the west of the Azores. All this intuition of which so much transcendental rubbish is merchanted is no more and no less than intelligence. . . . Women decide the larger questions of life correctly and quickly, not because they are lucky guessers, not because they are divinely inspired, not because they practice a magic inherited from savagery, but simply and solely because they have sense. They see at a glance what most men could not see with searchlights and telescopes; they are at grips with the essentials of a problem before men have finished debating its mere externals. They are the supreme realists of the race. . . . Men, too, sometimes have brains. But that is a rare, rare man, I venture, who is as steadily intelligent, as constantly sound in judgement, as little put off by appearances, as the average woman of forty-eight.

— H. L. MENCKEN, *In Defense of Women,*
PART I, "THE FEMININE MIND," 1922

∾ *Sapient folk wisdom provided profound insights into the male mentality.*

"Did you hear about the baby who was born bisexual?"
"What about him?"
"He was born with both a penis and a brain."

•

"Did you hear about the man who won the gold medal at the Olympics?"
"What about him?"
"He had it bronzed."

•

Diamonds are a girl's best friend. Dogs are a man's best friend. Now you know which sex is smarter.

•

A man became worried about his baldness. A friend recommended that he get a transplant.
A month later he showed up with a heart on his head.

•

The neighbor said to the man, "You should pull your shades at night. Last night I saw you and your wife making love through the living-room window."

"Ha, ha," said the man. "The joke's on you. I wasn't even home!"

•

A man came home from work early one day and found his wife naked and panting on the bed. "Honey," she said, thinking quickly, "I think I'm having a heart attack!" While rushing to call the doctor, he nearly stumbled over his crying four-year-old, who told him there was a naked man in the closet. He ran to the closet, opened the door, and there was his best friend. "Damn it, Dave," he shouted, "Jill's having a heart attack and here you are scaring the hell out of the kids!" — U.S. JOKES, 1990s

☙ *Are "men" natural-born fools?*

There's nineteen men livin' in my neighborhood:
Eighteen of them are fools
          and the one ain't no doggone good.
                                        — BESSIE SMITH (1898–1937)

I'm not denyin' the women are foolish: God Almighty made 'em to match the men. — GEORGE ELIOT, *Adam Bede*, 1859

26

A man is one who loses his illusions first, his teeth second, and his follies last.   — HELEN ROWLAND, C. 1925

When he said we were trying to make a fool of him, I could only murmur that the Creator had beat us to it.

— ILKA CHASE (1905–1978)

The bitterest creature under heaven is the wife who discovers that her husband's bravery is only bravado, that his strength is only a uniform, that his power is but a gun in the hands of a fool.

— PEARL S. BUCK, "Love and Marriage,"
To My Daughters, With Love, 1967

Because men are simple, they are not physically capable of handling more than one task at a time. Women can easily cook dinner, feed the baby, and talk on the phone all at once. Were a man to try this, he would probably explode.

— ROSEANNE ARNOLD

∾ *Enlightened males never had trouble admitting the intellectual superiority of women.*

Women's advice is worthless, but he who does not take it is a fool.

— SPANISH PROVERB

A woman's guess is much more accurate than a man's certainty.
— RUDYARD KIPLING, "Three and—an Extra,"
Plain Tales from the Hills, 1888

Verily, men do foolish things thoughtlessly, knowing not why;
but no woman doeth aught without a reason.

— GELETT BURGESS, *The Maxims of Methuselah,* 1907

There was, I think, never any reason to believe in any innate superiority of the male, except his superior muscle.

> — Bertrand Russell, "Ideas That Have
> Harmed Mankind," *Unpopular Essays,* 1950

We don't just need a new generation of leadership, we need a new gender of leadership.

> — Governor Bill Clinton, to the Women's Caucus of the
> Democratic National Convention, July 1992

There's a great woman behind every idiot.

> — John Lennon (1940–1980)

It's relaxing to go out with my ex-wife because she already knows I'm an idiot.   — Warren Thomas

Even the wisest men make fools of themselves about women, and even the most foolish women are wise about men.

> — Theodor Reik, *The Need to Be Loved,* 1963

Though women have small force to overcome men by reason, yet have they good fortune to undermine them by policy [stratagem].

> — John Lyly, *Euphues, the Anatomy of Wit,* 1579

My toughest fight was with my first wife.   — Muhammad Ali

Woman is man's confusion!

> — Vincent of Beauvais, *Speculum Majus,* 13th century

MALE LOGIC

~ *What about the vaunted superiority of male logic?*

One of the things that politics has taught me is that men are not a reasoned or reasonable sex. — MARGARET THATCHER

I want to know why, if men rule the world, they don't stop wearing neckties. — LINDA ELLERBEE, *Move On,* 1991

Don't ever be completely masculine, because a superior woman is superior to her masculine colleagues. In you as a woman there are some exceptional qualities, but they would cease to be so attractive and so remarkable if you got too close to that other part of the human species that is *egoism personified*.
  — UNKNOWN, letter to Isabelle Eberhardt, 18TH CENTURY

Women want mediocre men, and men are working hard to be as mediocre as possible. — MARGARET MEAD, in *Quote,* MAY 15, 1958

Whatever women do they must do twice as well as men to be thought half as good. Luckily this is not difficult.
  — CHARLOTTE WHITTON, on becoming
  mayor of Ottawa, Ontario, 1963

I still believe women are the superior sex.
  — JANE FONDA, in the *Los Angeles Times,* 1989

If man is only a little lower than the angels, the angels should reform. — MARY WILSON LITTLE

·❦· *What about the New Sensitive Male we used to hear about?*

Beware of the man who praises women's liberation; he is about to quit his job.   — Erica Jong

Beware of men who cry. It's true that men who cry are sensitive to and in touch with feelings, but the only feelings they tend to be sensitive to and in touch with are their own.   — Nora Ephron

THE COUCH POTATO

·❦· *Are "men" capable of any feelings at all? Most experts agree they are not.*

The standard Western adult male is rendered incapable of being comfortable with emotional expression . . . being quite incapable of understanding what it is like to be someone else.
        — Janet Daley, British columnist, in *The Independent,* 1990

He . . . treats his emotions like mice that infest our basement or rats in the garage, as vermin to be crushed in traps or poisoned with bait.   — Marge Piercy, *Braided Lives,* 1982

All along, one of my major complaints was his absence from home, and even worse, his absence when he *was* home.
        — Sonia Johnson, *From Housewife to Heretic,* 1981

The male is a complete egocentric, trapped inside himself, incapable of empathizing or identifying with others, of love, friendship, affection or tenderness. He is a completely isolated unit, incapable of rapport with anyone. . . . He is a half-dead, unresponsive lump—consequently he is at best an utter bore. . . . Eaten up with guilt, shame, fears and insecurities and obtaining, if he's lucky, a barely perceptible physical feeling, the male is, nonetheless, obsessed with screwing. . . .

— VALERIE SOLANIS, *The S.C.U.M. Manifesto,* 1967

No wonder "men," before their obsolescence, were beset by feelings of doom and insecurity.

The classic function of the "warrior" helped men throughout history achieve a sense of confidence they needed to cope with women.

— PAGE SMITH, in the *San Francisco Chronicle,* NOVEMBER 17, 1991

I am a woman meant for a man, but I never met a man who could compete. —BETTE DAVIS (1908–1989)

Probably the only place where a man can feel really secure is in a maximum security prison, except for the imminent threat of release. — GERMAINE GREER

⌒ *It is when wallowing in apathy and sloth that man is most truly himself.*

For vacant hours of man's destructive leisure
Were sports invented of the barbarous kind;
But tempt not me to share thy cruel pleasure—
No sports are guiltless to the feeling mind.

Shall I, who cultivate the Muse's lays,
And pay my homage at Apollo's shrine,
Shall I to torpid angling give my days,
And change poetic wreaths for fishing-line?

Sit like a statue by the placid lake,
My mind suspended on a gudgeon's fate;
Transported if the silly fish I take,
Chagrined and weary, if it shuns the bait?
— ELIZABETH MOODY, "To a Gentleman Who Invited
Me to Go A-Fishing," 1798

Give a man a fish and you feed him for a day. Teach a man to fish, and you get rid of him on the weekends.   — UNKNOWN

The Couch Potato
Deep in the pillows he snuggles. A lump
My dedicated sofa chump.
Turn on the set. Start up the game.
Whatever the sport—it's all the same. . . .
There he lies, my chubby hubby,
Tracking every Met and Cubbie. . . .
Now and then he announces the score.

Of life at home he asks no more.
I pat him in passing and tell myself this,
One of us two has found perfect bliss.

— Vesle Fenstermaker

Any gal is gonna go out of her mind when she looks at her husband one day and realizes that she is not living with a man any longer. She is living with a reclining chair that burps.

— Roseanne Arnold

In like manner, in the room where he eats, on the floor lie the rinds of melons, bones, refuse, leaves of lettuce, all left there without ever being swept up. . . . The platters he washes as little as he can, and the dog licks and cleans them; the earthen pots are all greasy, go, look in what condition they are! Do you know how he lives? Like a beast.

— St. Bernadine of Siena, *Sermons*, 15th century

◦ *What women want; what men want:*

What Women Want: To be loved, listened to, desired, respected, needed, and trusted.

What Men Want: Tickets for the World Series.
— FEMINIST T-SHIRT SLOGAN, 1992

I want a man who's kind and understanding. Is that too much to ask of a millionaire?
— ZSA ZSA GABOR

Myself, I either want to be gratifying my nerve endings with TV, sex, a car or beer, or I want to be taking a nap. Women seem to have a more diffuse agenda, involving all sorts of plans and people, and people getting together, and kids and families and more kids. And women, of course, never take naps.
— ERIC BOGOSIAN, in Playboy, AUGUST 1993

◦ *When "men" were still permitted to express themselves publicly, they vacillated between hooting obscenely at female strangers in the street and lapsing into a stunned silence.*

Most men are in a coma when they are at rest and mad when they act.
— EPICURUS (342?–270 B.C.), Letters, Principal
Doctrines, and Vatical Sayings

Women speak because they wish to speak, whereas a man speaks only when driven to speech by something outside himself—like, for instance, he can't find any clean socks.
— JEAN KERR, "How to Talk to a Man,"
The Snake Has All the Lines, 1960

36

Women like silent men. They think they're listening.
— Marcel Achard, in *Quote,* November 4, 1956

∾· *At the same time, too many of them tiresomely insisted on verbalizing their supposed thoughts.*

Men talk about what happened; women talk about what really happened. Men talk about what they are supposed to talk about; women talk about what really concerns them. Women are good listeners. . . . — Tina Brown, editor of *The New Yorker,*
in *Media Report to Women,* Winter 1991–92

A man is like a phonograph with half-a-dozen records. You soon get tired of them all; and yet you have to sit at a table whilst he reels them off to every new visitor.
— George Bernard Shaw, Preface to *Getting Married,* 1911

A healthy male adult bore consumes each year one and a half times his own weight in other people's patience.
— John Updike, "Confessions of a Wild Bore," 1965

Men will pay large sums to whores For telling them they are not bores.
— W. H. Auden, "New Year Letter," 1940

∙∾∙ *Whatever happened to the strong, silent type?*

Whatever happened to the strong, silent type? Today's man talks, talks, talks 'til we're blue in the face. And I fear there's no undoing the damage. The new old saying? Boys will be noise.

— Nina Malkin

∙∾∙ *Is there any significant difference between one man and another?*

CLONELY ONE: Interchangeable type of male available to heterosexual women; man named Gene very nearly chromosomally identical to all other men in sexist attitudes and behaviors; cheap carboniferous copy over whom women have been known to kill themselves. — Kate Musgrave, *Womb with Views,* 1989

Give but a grain of the heart's rich seed,
Confine some under cover.
And when love goes, bid him God-speed,
And find another lover.

— Countee Cullen, "Song in Spite of Myself,"
On These I Stand, 1947

A woman need know but one man well, in order to understand all men; whereas a man may know all women and understand not one of them. — Helen Rowland

☙ *Women have always understood male creatures better than the latter understood women.*

I was amused at what your Reverence said about your being able to sum up that woman as soon as you saw her! You cannot sum up women as easily as that! We make our confessions year in and year out, and even so our confessors are astonished to find out how little they have learnt about us.

— St. Theresa of Avila (1515–1582), letter to
P. Ambrosio Mariano de San Benito, October 21, 1576

Why are women so much more interesting to men than men are to women?
— Virginia Woolf (1882–1941)

A CREATURE OF VANITY

☙ *The vanity of the male animal rivals that of the Babylonian peacock-god.*

The arrogance of men, indeed,
comes full equipped with evil,
in promise and insistency,
the world, the flesh, the Devil.

— Sor Juana Inés de la Cruz, 1690

The male ego with few exceptions is elephantine to start with.
— Bette Davis, *The Lonely Life,* 1962

He was like a cock who thought the sun had risen to hear him crow.   — GEORGE ELIOT, *Adam Bede,* 1859

The fool shouts loudly, thinking to impress the world.
                              — MARIE DE FRANCE, 12TH CENTURY

Believe me, Mr. Pureheart, nothing makes a young man look more ridiculous than trying to look cleverer than everybody else. He is a great admirer of his humble self [she laughs]; and, as far as I know, the only one.
        — MISS LOTTIE in Luise Adelgunde Gottsched, *The Witling,* 1745

We were walking down the street. He looked into another girl's eyes, and just fell madly in love. She was wearing mirrored sun-glasses.   — RITA RUDNER

We had a lot in common. I loved him and he loved him.
                                    — SHELLEY WINTERS, 1952

⟡ *"Men" by no means disagree.*

No healthy male is ever actually modest. His conversation is one endless boast—often covert, but always undiluted.
                                          — H. L. MENCKEN

When I was young my vanity was such that when I went to a brothel I always picked the ugliest girl and insisted on making love to her in front of them all without taking my cigar out of my mouth. It wasn't any fun for me: I just did it for the gallery.
                                — GUSTAVE FLAUBERT (1821–1880)

Man is a marvelously vain, diverse, and undulating object. It is hard to found any constant and uniform judgment on him.

•

There is no man so decrepit whilst he has Methuselah before him who does not think he has still twenty years of life in his body.

•

Man is certainly crazy. He could not make a mite, yet he makes gods by the dozens.

— MICHEL DE MONTAIGNE, *Essays,* 1580

᠈᠋᠊᠄ *This universal male quality has the happy effect of making "men" easy to manage.*

If a man is vain, flatter. If timid, flatter. If boastful, flatter. In all history, too much flattery never lost a gentleman.

— KATHRYN CRAVENS, *Pursuit of Gentlemen*

Women have served all these centuries as looking-glasses possessing the magic and delicious power of reflecting the figure of man at twice its natural size.

— VIRGINIA WOOLF, *A Room of One's Own,* 1929

If you talk about yourself, he'll think you're boring. If you talk about others, he'll think you're a gossip. If you talk about him, he'll think you're a brilliant conversationalist.   — LINDA SUNSHINE

A man admires the woman who makes him think, but he keeps away from her. He likes the woman who makes him laugh. He loves the girl who hurts him. But he marries the woman who flatters him.

— Nellie B. Stull, in *Reader's Digest,* 1935

There is but one way for a woman to both hold onto her tyrant and at the same time to lighten her oppression: by flattering him shamelessly. . . . She must prostrate herself before him and say—"You are great, you are sublime, you are incomparable! You are more perfect than God. Your face is radiant; in your footsteps, nectar is distilled; you are without a single failing and every virtue is yours. No individual is your equal. . . ."

Immodest creature, you do not want a woman who will accept your faults, you want one who pretends that you are faultless—one who will caress the hand that strikes her and kiss the lips that lie to her.

— George Sand, *The Intimate Journal,* 1837

No man has ever lived that had enough
Of children's gratitude or woman's love.

— William Butler Yeats, "Vacillation," 1932

"GREAT MEN"

↜ *The ancient days of the patriarchy promoted the oxymoronic myth of "Great Men." But sapients always knew better.*

Mountains appear more lofty the nearer they are approached, but great men resemble them not at all in this particular.

— Marguerite Power, Countess of Blessington (1789–1849)

I have had my bellyful of great men. . . . In real life they are nasty creatures, persecutors, temperamental, despotic, bitter and suspicious.
— GEORGE SAND, *Correspondence,* Vol. II, 1895

A man who's too good for the world is no good for his wife.
— YIDDISH PROVERB

Heaven save me from the smartest man in the world, at least when he is a conceited fool.
— MISS LOTTIE in Luise Adelgunde Gottsched, *The Witling,* 1745

A man with big ideas is a hard neighbor to live with.
— MARIE VON EBNER-ESCHENBACH, *Aphorisms,* 1905

I fear nothing so much as a man who is witty all day long.
— MARIE DE SÉVIGNÉ

He has a brilliant mind until he makes it up.
— DAME MARGOT ASQUITH, *Autobiography,* 1923

Selected sapient commentary on individual Great Men:

If you weren't such a great man you'd be a terrible bore.
— MRS. WILLIAM GLADSTONE to her husband

He speaks to me as if I were a public meeting.
— QUEEN VICTORIA (1819–1901) on Gladstone

Henry Kissinger may have wished I had presented him as a combination of Charles de Gaulle and Disraeli, but I didn't . . . out of respect for de Gaulle and Disraeli. I described him as a cowboy because that is how he described himself. If I were a cowboy I would be offended. — ORIANA FALLACI, 1979

Sometimes when I look at my children I say to myself, "Lillian, you should have stayed a virgin."
— LILLIAN CARTER, mother of Jimmy and Billy,
in *Life* magazine, JANUARY 1981

Sure, Reagan promised to take senility tests. But what if he forgets? — LORNA KERR-WALKER, 1981

Henry James chews more than he bites off.
— MARIAN HOOPER ADAMS,
wife of Henry, c. 1880

I wish Frank Sinatra would just shut up and sing.
— LAUREN BACALL, to Barbara Walters

When you were quite a little boy somebody ought to have said "hush" just once.
— MRS. PATRICK CAMPBELL, letter to George Bernard Shaw, 1912

THE SAVAGE

❧ *The male's primitive nature, frustrated inarticulacy and baseless vanity go a long way toward explaining his universal predisposition to violence.*

War is menstrual envy!
— FEMINIST ANTIWAR SLOGAN

[Men are] a group sexually trained to woman-hating violence.
— CATHARINE MacKINNON, in *The New York Times*, DECEMBER 15, 1991

The only genetic superiority that men have is their capacity for violence, which in this age of preparation for total war has taken on an institutionalized form. We all need to be rescued from the computer-aimed nuclear phallus that kills without passion.
— GERMAINE GREER, *The Slag Heap Erupts*, 1970

⤞ *Some thinkers claimed that male violence* is *passion, and man's only passion, at that.*

There are only two kinds of men—the dead and the deadly.

— Helen Rowland

A woman who
has never been hit
by a man has
never been loved.
— Zsa Zsa Gabor,
in *Vanity Fair,*
December 1983

Scratch a lover, and find a foe!

— Dorothy Parker, *Enough Rope,* 1926

. . . a wicked man who is also eloquent
Seems the most guilty of them all. He'll cut your throat
As bold as brass, because he knows he can dress up murder
In handsome words.   — Medea, in Euripides, *Medea,* 431 b.c.

⤞ *The Macho Man:*

Some men are so macho they'll get you pregnant just to kill a rabbit.   — Maureen Murphy

46

Macho does not prove mucho. — ZSA ZSA GABOR

ᴖ· *Violence is the fundamental component of male nature.*

If a woman gets nervous, she'll eat or go shopping. A man will attack a country—it's a whole other way of thinking.
  — ELAYNE BOOSLER

I am more and more convinced
that man is a dangerous creature. . . .
  — ABIGAIL ADAMS, letter to John
    Adams, NOVEMBER 27, 1775

Eve was no danger to posterity but only to
herself; but the man Adam spread the infection
of sin to himself and to all future generations.
Thus Adam, being the author of all humans
yet to be born, was also the first cause of their
perdition.
  — ISOTTA NOGAROLA, letter to Lord Ludovico Foscarini, C. 1452

ᴖ· *Even "men" acknowledged the essential connection between masculinity and violence.*

Of all the animals on earth, none is so brutish as man when he
seeks the delirium of coition.
  — EDWARD DAHLBERG, *The Edward Dahlberg Reader,* 1967

Yet each man kills the thing he loves,
   By each let this be heard,
Some do it with a bitter look,
   Some with a flattering word.
The coward does it with a kiss,
   The brave man with a sword!
       — Oscar Wilde, *The Ballad of Reading Gaol,* 1898

For the first year of marriage I had a basically bad attitude. I tended to place my wife underneath a pedestal.   — Woody Allen

Becoming masculine does not involve simple "imprinting." One has to *dare* to do certain activities which are dangerous and can be painful. There is nothing automatic about fighting.
       — Norman Mailer

Men are not human beings, they are human doings.
       — Warren Farrell, Ph.D., late 1960s

THE "GENTLEMAN"

We will learn more about the male equivalency of sex and violence later on. Meanwhile, a few words from dissidents ("gentlemen"):

A gentleman is someone who never strikes a woman without provocation.   — H. L. Mencken

I've never struck a woman in my life, not even my own mother.
       — W. C. Fields (1879–1946)

48

I am a gentleman: I live by robbing the poor.
— George Bernard Shaw, *Man and Superman,* 1903

⌒ *While the occasional collaborationist may have suggested*

It is possible that blondes also prefer gentlemen.
— Mamie Van Doren

⌒ *...it was well known that even "gentlemen" were not to be trusted.*

A gentleman is a patient wolf.   — Henrietta Tiarks

A fox is a wolf who sends flowers.
— Ruth Weston, in the *New York Post,* 1955

He is every other inch a gentleman.

— REBECCA WEST (1892–1983)

It is a gentleman's first duty to remember in the morning who it was he took to bed with him.

— DOROTHY L. SAYERS (1893–1957)

A CREATURE OF SEX

↬ *Every man is obsessed with sex.*

He'll swim a river of snot, wade nostril deep through a mile of vomit, if he thinks there'll be a friendly pussy awaiting him. He'll screw a woman he despises, any snaggle-toothed hag, and furthermore, pay for the opportunity. And he'll also screw babies and corpses. — VALERIE SOLANIS, *The S.C.U.M. Manifesto,* 1967

Give a man a free hand and he'll run it all over you.

— MAE WEST (1892–1980)

A man is as young as the women he feels.

— UNKNOWN

Outside every thin woman is a fat man trying to get in.

— KATHARINE WHITEHORN
(and others)

∾ *A sapient anthropologist explains the phenomenon of male attractiveness:*

The beautiful coloring of male birds and fishes, and the various appendages acquired by males throughout the various orders below man, and which so far as they themselves are concerned, serve no other useful purpose than to aid them in securing the favours of the females, have by the latter been turned to account in the process of reproduction. The female made the male beautiful that *she might endure his caresses.*

— Eliza Burt Gamble, *The Sexes in Science and History,* c. 1910

∾ *To preserve their phallohegemonic dominance, "men" often pretended to enjoy sex.*

I believe that sex is the most beautiful, natural, and wholesome thing that money can buy. — Steve Martin

It takes no skill, lasts less than a minute and you can brag to your friends how terrific you were. No wonder men love it.

— Jim Mullen, reflecting on the perils and rewards of bungee jumping, in *Playboy,* July 1993

Give me chastity and continence, but not yet!

— St. Augustine, *Confessions,*

5th century a.d.

I will find you twenty lascivious turtles ere one chaste man.
— WILLIAM SHAKESPEARE, *The Merry Wives of Windsor,* 1597

∾ As to the faithfulness of husbands . . .

People who are so dreadfully devoted to their wives are so apt, from mere habit, to get devoted to other people's wives as well.
— JANE WELSH CARLYLE, on her
faithless husband, c. 1860

A man's heart may have a secret sanctuary where only one woman may enter, but it is full of little anterooms which are seldom vacant. — HELEN ROWLAND

Husbands are chiefly good lovers when they are betraying their wives.
— MARILYN MONROE

I don't think there are any men who are faithful to their wives.
— JACQUELINE KENNEDY ONASSIS

I wouldn't trust my husband with a young woman for five minutes, and he's been dead for 25 years.
— BRENDAN BEHAN'S MOTHER

Lady, Lady, should you meet
One whose ways are all discreet,
One who murmurs that his wife

Is the lodestar of his life,
One who keeps assuring you
That he never was untrue,
Never loved another one . . .
Lady, lady, better run!
— DOROTHY PARKER, "Social Note," 1926

When a rogue kisses you, count your teeth.
— HEBREW PROVERB

 They were rogues, all right!

The kiss originated when the first male reptile licked the first female reptile, implying in a subtle, complimentary way that she was as succulent as the small reptile he had for dinner the night before.
— F. SCOTT FITZGERALD, *The Crack-Up,* 1945

It is easier for a sieve to hold water than for a woman to trust a man. — LEBANESE PROVERB

Trust not a man; we are by nature false,
Dissembling, subtle, cruel and unconstant.
— THOMAS OTWAY, *The Orphan,* 1680

I regard men as a pleasant pastime but no more dependable than the British weather.
— ANNA RAEBURN, British therapist,
on BBC–TV, 1990

He promised me earrings, but he only pierced my ears.

— Arabic proverb

✦ *"Men" always acknowledged their barnyard propensity.*

I know many married men, I even know a few happily married men, but I don't know one who wouldn't fall down the first open coal-hole running after the first pretty girl who gave him a wink.

— George Jean Nathan
(1882–1958)

Eighty percent of married men cheat in America. The rest cheat in Europe.

— Jackie Mason

No man worth having is true to his wife, or can be true to his wife, or ever was, or ever will be so.

— Sir John Vanbrugh, *The Relapse,* 1607

Young men want to be faithful, and are not; old men want to be faithless, and cannot.

— Oscar Wilde, *The Picture of Dorian Gray,* 1891

A husband is a man who wishes he had as much fun when he is out as his wife thinks he does. — ANON.

Let us allow some of the creatures to attempt to defend themselves.

I am a strict monogamist: it is twenty years since I last went to bed with two women at once, and then I was in my cups and not myself. — H.L. MENCKEN

My wife was in labor with our first child for thirty-two hours and I was faithful to her the whole time. — JONATHAN KATZ

If there were no husbands, who would look after our mistresses? — GEORGE MOORE, 1888

THE RISIBLE MALE

A gentleman once asked, "Why do women so utterly lack a sense of humor?" The answers:

God did it on purpose, so that we may love you men instead of laughing at you. — MRS. PATRICK CAMPBELL, C. 1910

When God created man, She was only joking. — ANON.

Nothing spoils a romance so much as a sense of humour in the woman. — OSCAR WILDE, *A Woman of No Importance*, 1893

If men knew what women laughed about, they would never sleep with us. — ERICA JONG

A couple gets married, and on the wedding night the husband pulls down his pants and asks his new bride, "Now what's this?" She says, "That's a wee-wee." He says, "No, that's a cock." She says, "No, that's a wee-wee." He says, "No, darling, from now on you call that a cock." She says, "No, darling, I've seen lots of cocks and that's a wee-wee."

— U.S. JOKE, 1970s

One cannot always be laughing at a man without now and then stumbling on something witty.

— JANE AUSTEN, *Pride and Prejudice,* 1813

Men are frightened by women's humor because they think that when women are alone they're making fun of men. This is perfectly true. But they think we're making fun of their equipment when in fact there are so many more interesting things to make fun of—such as their value systems. Or the way they act when they're sick.

— NICOLE HOLLANDER, to Regina Barreca, 1989

✎ *But when you come right down to it, what is the most amusing spectacle of all?*

... the male genital, the visible doodle, the tag of flesh ... the tremulous dangling thing ... his tassel ... the pork sword....

— GERMAINE GREER, *The Politics of Female Sexuality,* 1970

56

I wonder why men can get serious at all.... They have this delicate long thing hanging outside their bodies which goes up and down by its own will.... Humor is probably something the male of the species discovered through his own anatomy.　— Yoko Ono, 1990

It is funny the two things most men are proudest of is the thing that any man can do and does in the same way, that is being drunk and being the father of their son.　— Gertrude Stein (1874–1946)

That the most intelligent, discerning and learned men, men of talent and feeling, should finally put all their pride in their crotch, as awed as they are uneasy at the few inches sticking out in front of them, proves how normal it is for the world to be crazy.
　— Françoise Parturier, *Open Letter to Men,* 1968

If the world were a logical place, men would ride side-saddle.
　— Rita Mae Brown, *Sudden Death,* 1983

A man is two people, himself and his cock. A man always takes his friend to the party. Of the two, the friend is the nicer, being more able to show his feelings.
　— Beryl Bainbridge

The penis is the only muscle man has that he cannot flex. It is also the only extremity that he cannot control.... But even worse, as it affects the dignity of its owner, is its seeming obedience to that inferior thing, woman. It rises at the sight or even at the thought of a woman.
　— Elizabeth Gould Davis, *The First Sex,* 1971

57

❧ *They never denied that their dingle-dangle transforms them into clowns.*

The biggest, strongest, most powerful men can be reduced by sex to imps. — Isaac Bashevis Singer (1904–1991)

When the prick stands up, the brain lies buried in the ground. — Yiddish proverb

I had often looked at my penis and thought, *"You moron."* — Paul Theroux, *My Secret History,* 1989

What would ye, ladies? It was ever thus.
Men are unwise and curiously planned. — James Elroy Flecker, *Hassan,* 1924

TEST YOUR KNOWLEDGE:
THE MALE MIND

What has an I.Q. of seven?
   Eight men.

•

What do you call a man with half a brain?
   Gifted.

•

Why are men happy?
   Because ignorance is bliss.

•

Why don't women have penises?
  Because women think with their brains.

•

What do you call that useless flap of skin at the end of a penis?
  A man.

•

Why are most blonde jokes one-liners?
  So men can understand them.

•

What's the difference between a penis and a prick?
  A penis is what a man uses to make babies, and a prick is the
  rest of him.

•

How many men does it take to pop popcorn?
  Three. One to hold the pan and two others to show off by
  shaking the stove.

•

How many men does it take to change a lightbulb?
  Five. One to force it with a hammer and four to go out for
  more bulbs.

•

How many men does it take to screw in a lightbulb?
　Just one. They'll screw anything.

•

What is a man?
　A life-support system for a penis.

•

What did God say after creating man?
　"I can do better."

•

What animal do men most resemble?
　A dog, only less loyal.

•

What can't a man keep: a job, a budget, or a promise?
　All of the above.

•

Where do you find a man who's committed?
　In a mental hospital.

•

Why did the man put a quarter in his condom?
　Because if he can't come, he'll call.

•

What do you call a man with his hands handcuffed behind his back?

Trustworthy.

•

Why does a man have a clean conscience?

Because it's never used.

•

What are two reasons why men don't mind their own business?

1. No mind.   2. No business.

•

Why is psychoanalysis a lot quicker for a man than for a woman?

Because when it's time to go back to childhood, he's already there.

•

Why do psychiatrists charge men half-price?

They have only half a brain to analyze.

•

What does a man consider a seven-course meal?

A six-pack and a hot dog.

•

What do you call an intelligent man in America?

A tourist.

•

What do you give the man who has everything?
   Penicillin.

•

Why is a dog man's best friend?
   Because a dog won't tell on him.

•

Why do men get only half an hour for lunch?
   So their bosses won't have to retrain them.

•

Why do doctors slap newborn babies on the back?
   So the penises will fall off the smart ones.

•

What do you call a man who's just lost 90% of his brains?
   Newly divorced.

•

What's the fastest way to lose 180 pounds?
   Throw the bum out.

•

How many men does it take to change a lightbulb?
  None. Every man knows that if he puts it off long enough, a woman will take care of it.

•

What's the best way to force a man to do sit-ups?
  Put the TV remote control between his toes.

•

What's the most exercise a man gets at the beach?
  Sucking in his gut when a bikini walks by.

•

What won't a man stand for?
  A pregnant woman on a bus.

•

What happened to the man who cleaned out his ears?
  His head caved in.

•

What happened to the man who put Odor-Eaters in his shoes?
  He disappeared.

•

How could Will Rogers say, "I never met a man I didn't like?"
  He never had to date one.

•

Why were men given larger brains than dogs?
  So they wouldn't hump women's legs at cocktail parties.

•

Why do men like masturbation?
  It's sex with someone they love.

•

What do you have when you have two little balls in your hand?
  A man's undivided attention.

•

What is a man's idea of a serious commitment?
  "OK, I'll stay the night."

•

Why do men name their penises?
  So they can be on a first-name basis with the person who makes 95% of their decisions.

•

What does a man call love?
An erection.

WHY IS A MAN LIKE . . .

. . . a beer bottle?
They're both empty from the neck up.

. . . decaffeinated coffee?
No active ingredients.

. . . bread?
They're both easier to take when you butter them up.

. . . soap?
When they get in hot water, they disappear.

. . . modern art?
Hard to understand and not really worth the effort.

. . . a baby?
A loud noise at one end and no sense of responsibility at the other.

. . . a vending machine?
They both take your money, but half the time they won't work.

. . . a riding stable?
Both are either vacant or full of shit.

. . . an air bag?
They open up only under pressure.

. . . the weather?
Nothing can be done to change either one of them.

. . . a laxative?
They both irritate the shit out of you.

AND WHAT IS THE DIFFERENCE
BETWEEN A MAN AND . . .

. . . a whale?
A whale mates for life.

. . . a government bond?
Bonds eventually mature.

. . . a savings account?
A savings account at least pays you a little interest.

. . . money?
Money talks.

. . . a new dog?

After a year, the dog is still excited to see you.

. . . a condom?

Condoms are no longer thick and insensitive.

. . . yogurt?

Yogurt has culture.

. . . E.T.?

E.T. phoned home.

. . . a catfish?

One is a bottom-feeding scum-sucker and the other is a fish.

— U.S., British, Canadian and Australian jokes, 1991–1993

Training the Male

∽· *Traditional sapient culture employed a variety of techniques for successful man-training.*

HELLO, SUCKER!

∽· *As long as "men" continue to exist, it is a fact of life that women create them. This responsibility proved an awesome burden in the days when they still dwelt freely among us.*

A good man doesn't just happen. They have to be created by us women. A guy is a lump like a doughnut. So, first you gotta get rid of all the stuff his mom did to him. And then you gotta get rid of all that macho crap that they pick up from beer commercials. And then there's my personal favorite, the male ego.

—ROSEANNE ARNOLD

One thing she has noticed about married women, and that is how many of them have to go about creating their husbands. They have to start ascribing preferences, opinions, dictatorial ways. Oh, yes, they say, my husband is very particular. He won't touch turnips. He won't eat fried meat. (Or he will only eat fried meat.) He likes me to wear blue (brown) all the time. He can't stand organ music. He hates to see a woman go out bareheaded. He would kill me if I took one puff of tobacco. This way, bewildered, sidelong-looking men are made over, made into husbands, heads of households.

—ALICE MUNRO, *Friend of My Youth,* 1990

There isn't a wife in the world who has not taken the exact measure of her husband, weighed him and settled him in her own mind, and knows him as well as if she had ordered him after designs and specifications of her own.

—CHARLES DUDLEY WARNER, *Backlog Studies,* 1873

I should like to see any kind of a man, distinguishable from a gorilla, that some good and very pretty woman could not shape a husband out of.

—OLIVER WENDELL HOLMES, SR., *The Professor at the Breakfast-Table,* 1860

A man is incomplete until he is married. Then he is finished.

—ZSA ZSA GABOR

❧ *Ease in training depended on selecting the right specimen.*

I require three things in a man: he must be handsome, ruthless, and stupid.

—DOROTHY PARKER

Chumps always make the best husbands. When you marry, Sally, grab a chump. Tap his forehead first, and if it rings solid, don't hesitate. All the unhappy marriages come from the husband's having brains. What good are brains to a man? They only unsettle him.

—P. G. WODEHOUSE, *The Adventures of Sally,* 1922

Any woman can fool a man if she wants to and if he's in love with her.

—AGATHA CHRISTIE (1891–1976)

A fool and his money are soon married.

—CAROLYN WELLS (and others)

He's a fool that marries; but he's a greater fool that does not marry a fool.   —WILLIAM WYCHERLY (1640–1716)

The weakness of men is the facade of strength; the strength of women is the facade of weakness.

—LAWRENCE DIGGS, *Transitions,* NOVEMBER–DECEMBER 1990

◦⟩ *When "men" were still permitted to run wild, the sapient-male relationship occasionally comprised a certain socioeconomic component.*

Hello, sucker!
> —TEXAS GUINAN, to her nightclub customers, 1930s

It is a sad woman who buys her own perfume.
> —LENA JEGER, in *The Observer* (London), NOVEMBER 20, 1955

Where's the man could ease a heart like a satin gown?
> —DOROTHY PARKER, "The Satin Dress," 1927

Watching her mother trying on her new fur coat, the daughter says unhappily, "Mom, do you realize some poor, dumb beast suffered just so you could have that coat?"

Her mother glares at her and says, "Don't talk about your father that way!"

•

A woman swathed in sable is confronted by an animal-rights activist. "Do you know how many wild animals had to die so you could get that coat?" demands the activist.

Replies the woman: "Do you know how many wild animals I had to *fuck* to get this coat?" —U.S. JOKES, 1980s

Keep cool and collect.
                    —MAE WEST, in *Belle of the Nineties,* 1934

When you are in love with someone you want to be near him all the time, except when you are out buying things and charging them to him.
        —MISS PIGGY, in Henry Beard, *Miss Piggy's Guide to Life,* 1981

Luxury is anything a husband needs.   —ANON.

A successful man is one who makes more money than his wife can spend. A successful woman is one who can find such a man.
                                        —LANA TURNER

No gold-digging for me . . . I take diamonds! We may be off the gold standard someday.   —MAE WEST

I never hated a man enough to give his diamonds back.

—Zsa Zsa Gabor, in *The Observer* (London),
August 28, 1957

⌒ *The story of the famous Kloppman diamond:*

A woman at a dinner party notices another woman's diamond
ring. She says: "My dear, what a magnificent diamond!"

"Yes, isn't it?" replies the second woman. "This is the famous
Kloppman diamond. Thirty-two carats and absolutely flawless.
Unfortunately, it comes with a dreadful curse."

"Really?" asks the first woman, intrigued. "And what is the
curse?"

"Mr. Kloppman."   —Myron Cohen, c. 1955

I've seen quite a few women wearing diamonds, but I never saw
a woman working in a diamond mine.   —Janna Ross, 1994

Diamonds are my service stripes.   —Mae West

I am a marvelous housekeeper. Every time I leave a man I keep
his house.   —Zsa Zsa Gabor

Trust your husband, adore your husband, and get as much as you
can in your own name.   —Joan Rivers, quoting her mother

God is love, but get it in writing.   —Gypsy Rose Lee

Love is a man's insane desire to become a woman's meal ticket.
— GIDEON WURDZ (and others)

Men have been trained and conditioned by women, not unlike
the way Pavlov conditioned his dogs, into becoming their slaves. As
compensation for their labors men are given periodic use of women's
vaginas. — ESTHER VILAR

All the young ladies said . . . that to be sure a love-match was the
only thing for happiness, where the parties could anyway afford it.
— MARIA EDGEWORTH, *Castle Rackrent,* 1800

"Repeat after me,
'I'm leaving you, Margaret.'"

 ✑ *What were some of the skills and techniques involved in man-training?*

The art of managing men has to be learned from birth. . . . It depends to some extent on one's distribution of curves, a developed instinct, and a large degree of feline cunning.

—MARY HYDE, *How to Manage Men*, 1955

Man is to be held only by the *slightest* chains; with the idea that he can break them at pleasure, he submits to them in sport.

—MARIA EDGEWORTH, *Letters of Julia and Caroline*, 1787

Will you walk into my parlor? said the Spider to the Fly;
'Tis the prettiest little parlor that ever you did spy.

—MARY HOWITT, "The Spider and the Fly," 1847

Men are like tea—the real strength and goodness are not properly drawn until they have been in hot water.

—LILLIE HITCHCOCK COIT (1843–1929)

Although there have been fleeting occasions when I have thought about tossing my beloved out the door, these urges were brought on by his idiot behavior and had nothing to do with my being a feminist. Frankly, it took me 17 years to get him semi house trained and I have no intention of starting over with some other man. . . . It happens to be my personal philosophy that if you give a man an inch of rope, he will tie you down with it, probably spread eagle to the bedposts. I am a feminist but I don't hate men. I do think you have to watch them very carefully though. They are like street cars, another comes along every 15 minutes, the trick is not to let one run over you.

   —FRANCES DECK, wiccan, letter in *Of a Like Mind,* SPRING 1993

If a woman's husband gets on her nerves, she should fly at him. If she thinks him too sweet and smarmy with other people, she should let him have it to his nose, straight out. She should lead him a dog's life, and never swallow her bile.

   —D. H. LAWRENCE, *Fantasia*
    of the Unconscious, 1922

WHAT IS A HUSBAND?

✧ *When the training program was successfully carried out, what, then, was a husband?*

A person who lays down the law to his wife and then accepts all her amendments.

•

A man who often finds that words flail him.

•

A hero in his own home until the company leaves.

—U.S. JOKES, 1950s

The Hen-Pecked Husband

Curst be the man, the poorest wretch in life,
The crouching vassal to a tyrant wife,
Who has no will but by her permission,
Who has not sixpence but in her possession,
Who must to her, his dear friends' secrets tell,
Who dreads a [bed-]curtain worse than ----:,
Were such a wife had fallen to my part,
I'd break her spirit, or I'd break her heart.
    —THE AMERICAN HUMORISTS (a male writing collective), c. 1900

Such jokesters may have laughed behind their cloak of anonymity, but the fact was . . .

A man's wife has more power over him than the state has.
    —RALPH WALDO EMERSON, *Journals,* 1836

I govern the Athenians, my wife governs me.   —THEMISTOCLES, C. 475 B.C.

Manny a man that cud rule a hundherd millyon sthrangers with an ir'n hand is careful to take off his shoes in th' front hallway whin he comes home late at night.
    —FINLEY PETER DUNNE, "Famous Men," 1919

The only really masterful noise a man ever makes in a house is the noise of his key, when he is still on the landing, fumbling for the lock.   —COLETTE (1873–1954)

   ✑ *Everyone knows that the domestication of males is essential to the maintenance of an orderly society.*

If it wasn't for women, men would still be hanging from trees.
—Marilyn Peterson

No society that domesticates too few men can have a stable social order.
—William Tucker, "Monogamy and Its Discontents," 1993

She knows her man, and when you rant and swear,
Can draw you to her *with a single hair*.
—Juvenal, *Satires,* c. A.D. 100, translated by John Dryden

Disguise our bondage as we will
'Tis woman, woman rules us still.
—Thomas Moore, "Sovereign Woman," c. 1850

❧ *Sapients always understood that it was ill-advised to allow even a trained male any freedom.*

Giving a man space is like giving a dog a computer: the chances are he will not use it wisely. — BETTE-JANE RAPHAEL

❧ *In addition, those who elected to interact with males never forgot*

THE RULES

1. The FEMALE always makes THE RULES.
2. THE RULES are subject to change at any time without prior notification.
3. No MALE can possibly know all THE RULES.
4. If the FEMALE suspects the MALE knows all THE RULES she must immediately change some or all of THE RULES.
5. The FEMALE is never wrong.
6. If the FEMALE is wrong, it is because of a flagrant misunderstanding which was a direct result of something the MALE did or said wrong.
7. If Rule 6 applies, the MALE must apologize immediately for causing the misunderstanding.
8. The FEMALE can change her mind at any time.
9. The MALE must NEVER change his mind without express written consent from the FEMALE.
10. The FEMALE has every right to be angry or upset at any time.

11. The MALE must remain calm at all times, unless the FEMALE wants him to be angry or upset.

12. The FEMALE must under no circumstances let the MALE know whether or not she wants him to be angry or upset.

13. The MALE is expected to mind read at all times.

14. The MALE who doesn't abide by THE RULES can't take the heat, lacks a backbone, and is a wimp.

15. Any attempt to document THE RULES could result in bodily harm.

16. If the FEMALE has PMS, all THE RULES are null and void.

17. The FEMALE is ready when she is ready. The MALE must be ready at all times.

> —ANON., Fax machine humor, c. 1990

MARRIAGE: THE VOICE OF EXPERIENCE

·✷· *Although marriage did offer women a certain amount of physical and financial security, as well as leisure and the myth of romance, it was not always unmitigated joy. Sapients who actually hazarded the tricky waters of matrimony remarked:*

I married beneath me. All women do.

> —LADY NANCY ASTOR (1879–1964)

The trouble with some women is that they get all excited about nothing—and then marry him. 　　　　　　　—CHER

Marrying a man is like buying something you've been admiring for a long time in a shop window. You may love it when you get it home, but it doesn't always go with everything else in the house.

—JEAN KERR, "The Ten Worst Things About a Man," *The Snake Has All the Lines,* 1960

It is true that I never should have married, but I didn't want to live without a man. Brought up to respect the conventions, love had to end in marriage. I'm afraid it did. —BETTE DAVIS, *The Lonely Life,* 1962

✑ *What's love got to do with it?*

Love, the strongest and deepest element in all life, the harbinger of hope, of joy, of ecstasy; love, the defier of all laws, of all conventions; love, the freest, the most powerful moulder of human destiny; how can such an all-compelling force be synonymous with that poor little State and Church-begotten weed, marriage?

—EMMA GOLDMAN, "Marriage and Love," c. 1910

A girl must marry for love, and keep on marrying until she finds it. —ZSA ZSA GABOR

Marriage is a souvenir of love.

—Helen Rowland

All that is good and commendable now existing would continue to exist if all marriage laws were repealed tomorrow. . . . I have an inalienable constitutional and natural right to love whom I may, to love for as long or as short a period as I can, and to change that love every day if I please!

—Victoria Woodhull, 1871

Love is the dawn of marriage, and marriage is the sunset of love.

—Anon.

Harmony before Matrimony

By the time you swear you're his,
  Shivering and sighing,
And he vows his passion is
  Infinite, undying—
Lady, make a note of this:
  One of you is lying.

—Dorothy Parker, "Unfortunate Coincidence," 1926

There are men I could spend eternity with. But not this life.

—Kathleen Norris, "Blue Mountain," 1981

    Did marriage have anything to do with sex?

Personally I know nothing about sex because I've always been married.   —Zsa Zsa Gabor, in *The Observer* (London), 1987

MATRIMONIAL HARMONICS

⌇ Sapient folk wisdom carefully analyzed the marriage-sex nexus.

A woman was complaining to her best friend over brunch. "Every time my husband climaxes, he lets out an ear-splitting yell."

"That doesn't sound all that bad to me," said her friend. "As a matter of fact, it would kind of turn me on."

"It would me too," said the first woman, "if only it didn't keep waking me up!"

•

Q: When does a woman stop masturbating?
A: After the divorce.

•

HUSBAND: What can I do to make sex better for you?
WIFE: Leave town.

•

HUSBAND: Let's go out and have some fun tonight.
WIFE: All right, but if you get home before I do, leave the door
     unlocked.

•

HUSBAND: Honey, I have some good news and some bad news.
          First, I've decided to run off with Gloria.
WIFE: No kidding! What's the bad news?

•

THERAPIST: Why don't you try using a little imagination when
          you make love to your husband?
WIFE: You mean imagine it's good?

•

A husband and wife were fighting about their sex life. "You never even tell me when you're having an orgasm!" the man yelled.

"How can I?" she shot back. "You're never here!"

•

My husband added some magic to our marriage. He disappeared.

•

Do you know what it means to come home to a man who'll give you a little love, a little affection, a little tenderness?

It means you're in the wrong house.

•

Yesterday I got a real nice used car for my husband.

I've seen your husband. It sounds like you got a good deal.

—U.S., BRITISH, CANADIAN AND AUSTRALIAN JOKES, 1990s

I have always found husbands much more satisfying after marriage than during.　　　　　　　　　—PEGGY GUGGENHEIM

Accursed from birth they be
Who seek to find monogamy,
Pursuing it from bed to bed—
I think they would be better dead.

—DOROTHY PARKER, "Reuben's Children," *Sunset Gun,* 1928

It is one thing to enjoy a man's society for an hour or two now and then, and another to annex him permanently. . . . The worst trial I ever had to endure . . . was having a husband continually on my hands.

> —GERTRUDE ATHERTON, 19th-century murderess, in her
> autobiography, *Can Women Be Gentlemen?*, 1938

ᢙ *Advice to virgins:*

Is there a way to detect meanness [in a man]?

If a lover proposes a ride, note how he manages his horse. If he avoids this rock and that rut, and drives kindly and considerately, all is right; but if he lashes here and jerks there, or shows temper or tyranny, or especially swears, you may safely infer that when he has

you, too, fairly in matrimonial harness, he will drive you likewise. In other words, learn from mickles what muckles mean.

—Professor Orson Squire Fowler, "Advice to a Young Lady,"
c. 1870

∾ *The difference between the lover and the husband:*

A husband is a lover with a two-days' growth of beard, his collar off, and a bad cold in the head. —James Huneker

A husband is what is left of the lover after the nerve has been extracted. —Helen Rowland, *A Guide to Men*, 1922

One exists with one's husband—one lives with one's lover.
—Honoré de Balzac (1799–1850)

Marriage is a romance in which the hero dies in the first chapter.
—Anon.

A lover is a man who tries to be more amiable than it is possible for him to be. —Nicholas Roche Chamfort (1740–1794)

One of the surest signs that a woman is in love is when she divorces her husband. —Dolly Parton

I've been in love with the same man for twenty years. If my husband ever finds out, he'll kill me. —Anon.

Do not marry your lover, and do not take back the man you have divorced. —Arabic proverb

REPEATING THE FOLLY

Why did some sapients repeat the folly?

I didn't vant to be alone.

—HEDY LAMARR, on why she married five times

When a woman marries again it is because she detested her first husband. When a man marries again, it is because he adored his first wife. Women try their luck; men risk theirs.

—OSCAR WILDE, *The Picture of Dorian Gray,* 1891

✒ *The Wife of Bath, classic lusty fem:*

Praise God, of husbands I've had five,
Whose assets I've enjoyed the best
Of fleshly purse and treasure chest. . . .
    Welcome, Six, whene'er he come!
More carnal joys I won't shrink from.
When Five is from the world a-gone,
Six will marry me anon. . . .
    And tell me please to what conclusion
Were members made for generation
And so generously wrought?
You know they were not made for naught. . . .
    Why else in writing was it set
That man must yield his wife her debt?
With what then shall he make his payment
If not his own sweet instrument?

— "The Wife of Bath's Prologue" in Geoffrey
Chaucer, *The Canterbury Tales,* c. 1387–1400

✒ *What did marriage teach sapients about "men"?*

Husbands, at best, have little to do with "people." I know, because I have had a certain number of them.

— Aimée Crocker (1862–1941), married five times

There is so little difference between husbands you might as well keep the first.

•

I think every woman is entitled to a middle husband she can forget.　　　　　　　　　　　　　—ADELA ROGERS ST. JOHN

I've married a few people I shouldn't have, but haven't we all?
　　　　　　　　　　　　　　　　　　—MAMIE VAN DOREN

The first time you buy a house you see how pretty the paint is and buy it. The second time you look to see if the basement has termites. It's the same with men.　　　　　　　　—LUPE VELEZ, 1930s

Whenever you want to marry someone, go have lunch with his ex-wife.　　　　　　　　　　　　　　　—SHELLEY WINTERS

American husbands are the best in the world; no other husbands are so generous to their wives, or can be so easily divorced.
　　　　　　　　　　　　　　—ELINOR GLYN (1864–1943)

Love the quest; marriage the conquest; divorce the inquest.
　　　　　—HELEN ROWLAND, *Reflections of a Bachelor Girl,* 1909

You never really know a man until you divorce him.
　　　　　　　　　　　　　　　　　　　—ZSA ZSA GABOR

In our family we don't divorce our men—we bury them.
　　　　　　　　　　　　　　—RUTH GORDON (1896–1985)

❧ *Dorothy Parker's second husband, Alan Campbell, died of an overdose of sleeping pills. Lillian Hellman reported that as his body was being taken out to the coroner's automobile, Mrs. Jones, an acquaintance who had liked Alan, rushed up to Parker and gushed, "Oh, Dottie, I am so sorry. Tell me, dear, what can I do for you?"*

"Get me a new husband," Dottie said.

There was a silence, but before those who were left could laugh, Mrs. Jones said, "I think that is the most callous and disgusting remark I ever heard in my life."

Dottie turned to look at her, sighed, and said gently, "So sorry. Then run down to the corner and get me a ham and cheese on rye and tell them to hold the mayo."

— LILLIAN HELLMAN, *An Unfinished Woman,* 1969

MARRIAGE VS. HAPPINESS

❧ *From the invention of Romantic Love in the 13th century until the Glorious Revolution of our own time, many confused marriage with happiness. Whoever said one had anything to do with the other?*

Happiness in marriage is entirely a matter of chance.

— JANE AUSTEN, *Pride and Prejudice,* 1813

Marriage is a lottery in which men stake their liberty, and women their happiness.

— VIRGINIE DE RIEUX, 17TH CENTURY

A happy marriage is when they are both in love with him.

— ANON.

Men are monopolists
   of "stars, garters, buttons
      and other shining baubles"—
   unfit to be the guardians
   of another person's happiness.
                              —MARIANNE MOORE,
                                 "Marriage," 1951

Very few modern women either like or desire marriage, especially after the ceremony has once been performed. Primarily, women wish attention and affection. Matrimony is something they accept when there is no alternative. Really, it is a waste of time, and hazardous, to marry them.
                              —HELEN LAWRENSON, "In Defense of the
                                 American Gigolo," *Esquire,* JANUARY 1930

Wait until a woman is married. . . . One no longer seeks to exalt their minds with romantic notions but to soil their hearts with cold jests on everything they have been taught to respect.
                              —GERMAINE DE STAËL, *Letters on the Works and
                                 Character of J.-J. Rousseau,* 1788

Nuns and married women are equally unhappy, if in different ways.   —QUEEN CHRISTINA OF SWEDEN, *Maxims,* c. 1660

What a happy state must a young woman imagine herself entering into, where she is to be lov'd, honour'd, cherish'd, nay, even worshiped; she has a protector till the hour of death, who . . . endows her with his fortune, and promises all that at the altar. . . .

94

No sooner is the honeymoon expir'd but the fawning servant turns a haughty lord: Instead of honouring his wife, 'tis odds if he treats her with common civility; he shall tell her, to her face, he wishes her death, in order to marry another....

As for our being endow'd with the worldly goods of our husbands, 'tis known they are so little apt to share with us, that it has always been found necessary, in a marriage-settlement, to stipulate for pin-money....

A woman of spirit, who is married to a sordid disagreeable wretch, has nothing to do but make him a cuckold; and then welcome thrice dear liberty: Yet methinks the husbands should, in justice, return to their wives, when they abandon them, the dowry they brought with them.

—LAETITIA PILKINGTON, *Memoirs,* c. 1750

Being married was like having a hippopotamus sitting on my face, Mrs. Brown. No matter how hard I pushed or which way I turned, I couldn't get up. I couldn't even breathe.... Hippopotamuses aren't all bad. They are what they are. But I wasn't meant to have one sitting on my face.

—FAITH SULLIVAN, *The Cape Ann,* 1988

Surely, of all creatures that have life and will, we women
Are the most wretched. When, for an extravagant sum,
We have bought a husband, we must then accept him as
Possessor of our body. This is to aggravate
Wrong with worse wrong....

>>> If a man grows tired
Of the company at home, he can go out, and find
A cure for tediousness. We wives are forced to look
To one man only. And, they tell us, we at home
Live free from danger, they go out to battle: fools!
I'd rather stand three times in the front line than bear
One child. ——MEDEA, in Euripides, *Medea,* 431 B.C.

A GREAT INSTITUTION

❧ *Many sapients wisely elected to forgo the rewards and pleasures of matrimony.*

Marriage is a great institution, but I'm not ready for an institution.

——MAE WEST

I think marriage is a very alienating institution, for men as well as women; it's a very dangerous situation—dangerous for men, who find themselves trapped, saddled with wife and children to

96

support; dangerous for women, who aren't financially independent of men who can throw them out when they're forty; and very dangerous for children, because their parents vent all their frustrations and mutual hatred on them. The very words "conjugal rights" are dreadful. Any institution which solders one person to another, obliging people to sleep together who no longer want to, is a bad one.

—SIMONE DE BEAUVOIR, in *The New York Times Magazine,* JUNE 2, 1974

I can't mate in captivity.

—GLORIA STEINEM, on why she never married

I never married because I would have to give up my favorite hobby.   —MAE WEST

Not all women are fools. Some are single.

—FEMINIST SLOGAN (bumper sticker), 1987

I think, therefore I'm single.   —LIZ WINSTON

It was so cold I almost got married.

—SHELLEY WINTERS, in *The New York Times,* APRIL 29, 1956

A man is an accessory, like a pair of earrings. It may finish the outfit, but you don't really need it to keep you warm.

—ROSEMARY MITTELMARK, 1994

I'd rather be a free spirit and paddle my own canoe.

—LOUISA MAY ALCOTT, "Happy Women" (essay), 1868

A woman without a man is like a fish without a bicycle.

—FEMINIST SLOGAN, variously attributed

If you want to sacrifice the admiration of many men for the criticism of one, go ahead, get married.

—KATHARINE HEPBURN, quoting her mother,

KATHARINE HOUGHTON HEPBURN, 1928

I am a lioness
and will never allow my body
to be anyone's resting place.
But if I did,
I wouldn't yield to a dog—
and O! the lions I've turned away!

—'AISHA BINT AHMAD AL-QURTUBIYYA,
Spanish-Arabic poet, 10TH CENTURY

I would rather be a beggar and single, than a Queen and married. . . . I should call the wedding ring the yoke ring.

—QUEEN ELIZABETH I of England (1533–1603)

A young man asked me: "What in your opinion *is* the ideal husband?" I cast about hastily in my mind and then replied: "Why—no husband at all."

—GERTRUDE ATHERTON, 19th-century murderess, in her
autobiography, *Can Women Be Gentlemen?,* 1938

Men have always been afraid that women could get along without them. —MARGARET MEAD (1901–1978)

꙳ *By the 18th century, the institution of matrimony was already falling into disrepute.*

To speak plainly, I am very sorry for the forlorn state of matrimony, which is as much ridiculed by our young ladies as it used to be by young fellows: in short, both sexes have found the inconvenience of it, and the appellation of rake is as genteel in a woman as a man of

quality; it is no scandal to say Miss ———, the maid of honour, looks very well now she is up again, and poor Biddy [Widow] Noel has never been quite well since her last confinement. You may imagine we married women look very silly; we have nothing to excuse ourselves but that it was done a while ago and we were very young when we did it. This is the general state of affairs.

—LADY MARY WORTLEY MONTAGU, 1723

It is a happy thing to be a mere blank, and to be able to pursue one's own whims where they lead, without having a husband and half a hundred children at hand to tease and control a poor woman who wishes to be free.

—MARY WOLLSTONECRAFT, letter to Jane Arden, 1782

Wife and servant are the same,
But only differ in the name. . . .
Value yourselves, and men despise:
You must be proud, if you'll be wise.

—LADY MARY CHUDLEIGH, *To the Ladies,* 1703

As to the disgrace supposedly attendant upon being an old maid:

If a woman hasn't met the right man by the time she's 24, she may
be lucky.   —DEBORAH KERR

In this happy life let me remain
Fearless of twenty-five and all its train
Of slights or scorns, or being call'd Old Maid,
Those goblins which so many have betray'd.

—JANE BARKER, "A VIRGIN LIFE," 1688

Being an old maid is like death by drowning, a really delightful sensation after you cease to struggle.   —EDNA FERBER (1887–1968)

Ↄ At one time, quaint as it now seems, women married for the sake of maternity. An early feminist male asked:

What woman in her senses would tie herself up in the fetters of matrimony, if it were not that she desires to be a mother of children, to multiply her kind, and, in short, have a family?

If she did not, she would be next to a lunatic to marry, to give up her liberty, take a man to call master, and promise when she takes him to honour and obey him. What! Give herself away for nothing! Mortgage the mirth, the freedom, the liberty, and all the pleasures of her virgin-state, the honour and authority of being her own, and at her own dispose, and all this to be a barren doe, a wife without children; a dishonor to her husband and a reproach to herself! Can any woman in her wits do thus?

—DANIEL DEFOE, *Conjugal Lewdness,* 1727

Of course, everybody knows that the greatest thing about Motherhood is the "Sacrifices," but it is quite a shock to find out that they begin so far ahead of time.

—ANITA LOOS, *A Mouse Is Born,* 1951

Ↄ Medieval antimarriage counselors relied on ridicule and rhetoric to dissuade young women from the toils and horrors of matrimony.

Now thou art wedded, and from so high estate alighted so low ... into the filth of the flesh, into the manner of a beast, into the thraldom of a man, and into the sorrows of the world. See now, what fruit it has . . . to cool thy lust with filth of the body, to have delight of thy fleshly will from man's intercourse: before God, it is a nauseous thing to think thereon, and to speak thereof is yet more nauseous. . . .

"Nay," thou wilt say, "as for that filth, it is nought; but a man's vigour is worth much, and I need his help for maintenance and food; of a woman's and a man's copulation, worldly welfare arises, and a progeny of fair children, that give much joy to their parents." . . . But I will show you that this is all made smooth with falsehood. . . .

When he is out, thou shalt await his homecoming with all sorrow, care, and dread. While he is at home, all thy wide dwellings seem too narrow for thee; his looking on thee makes thee aghast; his loathsome mirth and his rude behaviour fill thee with horror. He chideth and jaweth thee, as a lecher does his whore; he beateth thee and mauleth thee as his bought thrall and patrimonial slave.... What shall be the copulation between you in bed?...

Now let us proceed! Consider we what joy ariseth afterwards from gestation of children.... Thy ruddy face shall turn lean, and grow green as grass. Thine eyes shall be dusky, and underneath grow pale.... Within thy belly, the uterus shall swell and strut out like a water bag; thy bowels shall have pains, and there shall be stitches in thy flank, and pain rife in thy loins, heaviness in every limb. The burden of thy breast is on thy two paps, and the streams of milk which trickle out of thee. All thy beauty is overthrown with a withering. Thy mouth is bitter, and nauseous is all that thou chewest, and whatever thy stomach disdainfully receives, with lack of appetite, it throws up again. With all thy pleasure, and thy husband's joy, thou art perishing. Ah, wretch!...

After all this, there cometh from the child thus born, a crying and a weeping, that must about midnight make thee to waken.... And consider his late growing up, and his slow thriving; and that thou must ever have an anxiety in looking for the time when the child will perish, and bring on his mother sorrow upon sorrow....

Little knoweth a maiden of all this same trouble of wives' woe... nor of their work so nauseous.... And what if I ask besides, though it may seem silly, how the wife stands, that heareth, when she cometh in, her child scream, sees the cat at the meat, and the hound at the hide? Her cake is burning on the stone and her calf is sucking all the milk up, the pot is running into the fire, and the churl is scolding. Though it be a silly tale, it ought, maiden, to deter thee more strongly from marriage, for it seems not silly to her that trieth it.

—Anon., "Holy Maidenhood: A Debate on Marriage," 13th century

∾ *Later antimarriage rhetoric was slightly different. A Women's International Terrorist Conspiracy from Hell manifesto thundered:*

Marriage is a dehumanizing institution—legal whoredom for women. *Confront* the perpetrators of our exploitation as women. *Confront* the institutions which make us pawns in a male-dominated culture. . . . *Confront* the Bridal Fair, which encourages vulnerable young girls to be dutiful, uncomplaining, self-sacrificing, "loving" commodities on the marriage market, and well-packaged, fully automated, brand-conscious consumers. *Confront* the exhibitors of this commercial extravaganza: "Big Boys" of the world of business and finance who are at the same time enslaving and murdering our sisters and brothers in Asia, Africa, and Latin America. . . .

The Ritual is the Reality. Our wedding day is the "only" day in our lives. We commence, consummate, consume, and are consumed on that single day, having spent our childhood playing "house," and our adolescence filling hope chests with empty Hollywood–Madison Avenue dreams. . . .

Sisters! Let us confront the whoremakers at the Bridal Fair . . . but more important, confront and overthrow the institutions of marriage and capitalism which make such bridal fairs possible!

— W.I.T.C.H., "Confront the Whoremakers at the Bridal Fair," 1969

Sex

✧ *Some senti(person)talists claim to recall with fond nostalgia the days and nights of sex with men. Sadly, they delude themselves. Even before sex was universally recognized as a tool of oppression, many sapients agreed that it was . . .*

A BIG WASTE OF TIME

✧ *To begin with, it provided little, if any, pleasure to women.*

Sex is a pleasurable exercise in plumbing, but be careful or you'll get yeast in your drain tap. —RITA MAE BROWN

Coition, sometimes called "the little death," is more like a slight attack of apoplexy. —PAULINE SHAPLER, *The Feminist Guide,* 1974

An orgasm is just a reflex like a sneeze. —DR. RUTH WESTHEIMER

There's nothing colder than chemistry.

—ANITA LOOS, *Kiss Hollywood Goodby,* 1974

It's pitch, sex is. Once you touch it, it clings to you.

—MARGERY ALLINGHAM, *The Fashion in Shrouds,* 1938

Shopping is better than sex. If you're not satisfied after shopping, you can make an exchange for something you *really* like.

—ADRIENNE E. GUSOFF

Sex: That pathetic short-cut suggested by Nature the supreme joker as a remedy for our loneliness, that ephemeral communion which we persuade ourselves to be of the spirit when it is in fact only of the body—durable not even in memory!

—VITA SACKVILLE-WEST, *No Signposts in the Sea,* 1961

People spent altogether too much time thinking about it.

Sex is the tabasco sauce which an adolescent national palate sprinkles on every course in the menu.

—MARY DAY WINN, *Adam's Rib,* 1931

Sex annihilates identity, and the space given to sex in contemporary novels is an avowal of the absence of character.

—MARY MCCARTHY

That our popular art forms become so obsessed with sex has turned the U.S.A. into a nation of hobbledehoys; as if grown people don't have more vital concerns, such as taxes, inflation, dirty politics, earning a living, getting an education, or keeping out of jail. It's true that the French have a certain obsession with sex, but it's a particularly adult obsession. France is the thriftiest of all nations; to a Frenchman sex provides the most economical way to have fun. The French are a logical race.

—Anita Loos, *Kiss Hollywood Goodby,* 1974

꙳ *A sampling of personal testimonies:*

The truth is, sex doesn't mean that much to me now.

—Lana Turner

Ah, the sex thing. I'm glad that part of my life is over.

—Greta Garbo, to Sam Green, 1974

The only thing I miss about sex is the cigarette afterward.

—Florence King

After we made love he took a piece of chalk and made an outline of my body. —Joan Rivers

The important thing in acting is to be able to laugh and cry. If I have to cry, I think of my sex life. If I have to laugh, I think of my sex life. —Glenda Jackson

I am happy now that Charles calls on my bedchamber less frequently than of old. As it is, I now endure but two calls a week, and when I hear his steps outside my door I lie down on my bed, close my eyes, open my legs, and think of England.

—Lady Grace Hillingdon, *Journal,* 1912

Conventional sexual intercourse is like squirting jam into a doughnut.

—Germaine Greer

✆ *Do you suppose* unconventional *sex was any better?*

I've tried several varieties of sex. The conventional position makes me claustrophobic. And the others give me either a stiff neck or lockjaw.

—Tallulah Bankhead (1903–1968)

As for the topsy turvy tangle known as *soixante-neuf*, personally I have always felt it to be madly confusing, like trying to pat your head and rub your stomach at the same time.

—Helen Lawrenson, 1930s

Really that little dealybob is too far away from the hole. It should be built right in. —Loretta Lynn, on the female body

I'd like to talk briefly about oral sex. You *can* bite it off.

—Paxton Quigley, workshop leader,
"Women's Empowerment in the Nineties," 1993

∾ *We can attempt to understand some of the old sexual categories.*

Girls who put out are tramps. Girls who don't are ladies. This is, however, a rather archaic use of the word. Should one of you boys happen upon a girl who doesn't put out, do not jump to the conclusion that you have found a lady. What you have probably found is a lesbian. —Fran Lebowitz

Once you know what women are like, men get kind of boring. I'm not trying to put them down, I mean I like them sometimes as people, but sexually they're dull. —Rita Mae Brown

Either heterosexuality is the structure of oppression or it is not. . . . And I would like you to address the question . . . whether a good fuck is any compensation for getting fucked. And why everyone knows what that means.

—Catharine MacKinnon, *Feminism Unmodified,* 1987

Women complain about sex more than men. Their gripes fall into two major categories: (1) Not enough. (2) Too much.

— ANN LANDERS

MEN DON'T LIKE IT EITHER

⁓ *Even "men," in their rare moments of honesty, admitted that they too did not think much of sex.*

Sex is the biggest nothing of all time, as far as I'm concerned.

— ANDY WARHOL (1927–1987)

A man marries to have a home, but also because he doesn't want to be bothered with sex and all that sort of thing.

— W. SOMERSET MAUGHAM (1874–1965)

All this fuss about sleeping together. For physical pleasure I'd sooner go to my dentist any day.

— EVELYN WAUGH, *Vile Bodies,* 1930

The pleasure is fleeting, the position ridiculous, and the expense damnable.

— LORD PHILIP CHESTERFIELD (1694–1773), letter to his son

Mirrors and copulation are abominable because they increase the numbers of men. — JORGE LUIS BORGES

I love Mickey Mouse more than any woman I've ever known.

— WALT DISNEY (1901–1966)

I would rather score a touchdown than make love to the prettiest girl in the United States. — PAUL HORNUNG

I'd rather hit than have sex. — REGGIE JACKSON

Anyone who knows Dan Quayle knows that he would rather play golf than have sex any day. — MARILYN QUAYLE, 1981

When I have sex it takes four minutes. And that includes dinner and a show. — GILBERT GOTTFRIED

Sex drive: a physical craving that begins in adolescence and ends at marriage. — ROBERT BYRNE (quoting himself), in *The 637 Best Things Anybody Ever Said*, 1982

H. L. Mencken offered the definitive answer to those who foolishly asserted that "men" enjoyed sexual engagements, particularly of the extramarital variety:

The average man . . . is quite incapable of all these incandescent and intriguing divertissements. . . . I do not say, of course, that he is pure in heart, for the chances are that he isn't; what I do say is that, in the overwhelming majority of cases, he is pure in act, even in the face of temptation. And why? For several main reasons, not to go into minor ones. One is that he lacks the courage. Another is that he lacks the money. . . .

Even more effective than the fiscal barrier is the barrier of poltroonery. The one character that distinguishes man . . . indeed, is his excessive timorousness, his easy yielding to alarms, his incapacity

for adventure without a crowd behind him. In his normal incarnation he is no more capable of initiating an extra-legal affair . . . than he is of scaling the battlements of hell. He likes to think of himself doing it. . . . Often, indeed, this vanity leads him to imagine the thing done, and he admits by winks and blushes that he is a bad one. But at the bottom of all that tawdry pretense there is usually nothing more material than an oafish smirk. . . .

Finally, there is his conscience—the accumulated sediment of ancestral faint-heartedness in countless generations. . . . It may not worry him on ordinary occasions. . . . But the moment a concrete Temptress rises before him, her nose snow-white, her lips rouged, her eyelashes drooping provokingly . . . his conscience flares into function, and so finishes his business. First he sees difficulty, then he sees danger, then he sees wrong. The result? The result is that he slinks off in trepidation, and another vampire is baffled of her prey.

It is, indeed, the secret scandal of Christendom . . . that most men are faithful to their wives. You will travel a long way before you find a married man who will admit that *he* is, but the facts are the facts, and I am surely not one to flout them.

—H. L. MENCKEN, *In Defense of Women,*
Part IV, "Men and Sex," 1922

❦ *Indeed, for man, the ultimate tragedy was "the tragedy of the bedroom."*

Man survives earthquakes, epidemics, the horrors of disease, and all the agonies of the soul, but for all time his tormenting tragedy is, and will be, the tragedy of the bedroom.

—LEO TOLSTOY (1828–1910), to Maxim Gorki

∽ *How fortunate for him that he no longer need endure it!*

WOMEN WHO
CLAIMED TO ENJOY IT . . .

∽ *A startling number of sapients suffered under the bizarre delusion that they actually enjoyed the activity in question.*

Personally, I like sex and I don't care what a man thinks of me as long as I get what I want from him—which is usually sex.

— VALERIE PERRINE

I'd like to get married because I like the idea of a man being required by law to sleep with me every night.   — CARRIE SNOW

How do I feel about men? With my fingers!   — CHER

I wish I had as much in bed as I get in the newspapers.

— LINDA RONSTADT

I dress for women, and undress for men.

— ANGIE DICKINSON

She was always pleased to have him come and never sorry to see him go.   — DOROTHY PARKER, "Big Blonde," 1929

A hard man is good to find.   — ANON.

It's not the men in my life that counts—it's the life in my men.

·

I only like two kinds of men: domestic and imported.

·

A man in the house is worth two in the street.

·

I always did like a man in uniform. And that one fits you grand. Why don't you come up sometime and see me?

—MAE WEST, 1930s

Every woman should have a man for love, companionship and sympathy. Preferably at three different addresses. —ANON.

It is ridiculous to think you can spend your entire life with one person. Three is about the right number. Yes, I imagine three husbands would do it. —CLARE BOOTHE LUCE

Every woman deserves three lovers: an old one to take care of her, a young one to play with, and one her own age so she has someone to talk to. —JANNA ROSS, 1994

Had nature formed me of the other sex, I should certainly have been a rover.

—ABIGAIL ADAMS, letter to Isaac Smith, Jr., APRIL 20, 1771

It doesn't matter what you do in the bedroom as long as you don't do it in the street and frighten the horses.

—MRS. PATRICK CAMPBELL, C. 1910

He gave me a strange, tickling sensation that was, I confess, very enjoyable. . . . It was like being in the strong embrace of a man. I was more than comfortable.

> —AIMÉE CROCKER (1862–1941), on making love with a boa
> constrictor

. . . ACQUIESCED IN THEIR OWN OPPRESSION

My husband is German; every night I get dressed up like Poland and he invades me. — BETTE MIDLER

Every woman adores a Fascist,
The boot in the face, the brute
Brute heart of a brute like you.

> —SYLVIA PLATH, "Daddy," 1963

OLDER WOMAN/YOUNGER MAN

Shamefully, some sapients claimed to enjoy frisking about with "men" even after attaining what should have been the dignified state of middle age.

There was nothing more fun than a man!
   —DOROTHY PARKER, "The Little Old Lady in Lavender Silk," 1931

The only reason I would take up jogging is so that I could hear heavy breathing again. — ERMA BOMBECK

The lovely thing about being forty is that you can appreciate twenty-five-year-old men more.
— COLLEEN McCULLOUGH

Older woman younger man! Popular wisdom claims that this particular class of love affair is the most poignant, tender, poetic, exquisite one there is, altogether the choicest on the menu.
— DORIS LESSING

Twenty goes into sixty a lot more times than sixty goes into twenty.
— BETTE MIDLER, on older women marrying younger men vs. older men marrying younger women

The only men who are too young are the ones who write love letters in crayon, wear pajamas with feet, or fly for half fare.
— PHYLLIS DILLER

As a young man I used to have four supple members and one stiff one. Now I have four stiff and one supple.

—Duc Henri d'Aumale, 17th century

There ain't nothing' an ol' man can do but bring me a message from a young one.

•

I'd rather pay a young man's fare to California than tell an ol' man the distance.

—Jackie "Moms" Mabley (1894–1975)

꙳ *Blanche of Castile (1188–1252), Queen of France during her husband's, Louis VIII's, reign and twice regent for her son, Louis IX, was so powerful that some wags assumed she derived her potency from the manhood of the youthful Cardinal-Legate.*

Heu! morimur strati, vincti, mersi, spoliati;
Mentula legati nos facit ista pati.
(Alas, we die, beaten, chained, drowned, despoiled;
The legate's penis makes us suffer all this.)

—13th-century jest, from Matthew Paris, *Chronica majora*

WILDER, LOUDER AND MESSIER

A WOMAN TELLS MEN:

EVERYTHING YOU'VE ALWAYS WANTED TO KNOW ABOUT WOMEN
AND PROBABLY WON'T UNDERSTAND WHEN I EXPLAIN IT TO YOU

First of all, women want more sex than you do. They want it more often, with more variation of technique, and they want it to last longer than you can possibly bear. They also want it wilder, louder, and messier than you can ever imagine.

Even though you have been taught that women do not want to have sex as much as you do and women were taught that they shouldn't want it as much as you, you should not be surprised when you are lying in bed, besieged by financial worries and exhausted by a long day at work, and your girlfriend, who is every bit as exhausted and besieged as you are, is humping your thigh suggestively and running her fingers through your chest hair. . . .

Face it, guys, going to bed with a woman is a hell of a lot scarier than marching into an enemy minefield. The worst thing that can happen in a war is that you die. If you screw up in bed with a woman, she will tell you and everybody else who will listen what a fool you were. She'll laugh at you and make funny little gestures that indicate the size and shape of your weenie. And you can only *wish* you were dead.

Why take the chance?

But men have to be cool and pretend that they have nothing to worry about even though vaginas are hot and dark and gooshy and you're expected to put the most precious part of your body in there. No wonder you need massive amounts of drugs, alcohol, and emotional detachment in order to do it.

I'd like to clear one last thing up before I go off and eat an entire banana cream pie all by myself: Men and women do not get stuck together like dogs when they screw. . . .

If a woman could keep you inside her by clamping her vaginal muscles in an inextricable vicelike grip, you'd be there now.

—SHARY FLENNIKEN, "A Woman Tells Men," 1987

   Some expert advice:

Q. How long should sexual intercourse last?

A. This is an area of disagreement between the sexes. As a rule, women would like to devote as much time to foreplay and the sex act as men would like to devote to foreplay, the sex act, and building a garage. This tends to lead to dissatisfaction on the part of the woman, who is often just beginning to feel pleasantly sensuous when the man is off rooting around in the refrigerator to see if there's any Jell-O left.

Q. Well, isn't there some sensitive and caring and loving technique that a couple can use to slow the man down?

A. Yes. When the woman senses that the man is nearing climax, she can whisper: "The Internal Revenue Service called again today, but don't worry, I hung up on them."

—DAVE BARRY, *Dave Barry's Guide to Marriage and/or Sex,* 1987

Although I know he loves me,
Tonight my heart is sad;
His kiss was not so wonderful
As all the dreams I had.

—SARA TEASDALE, "The Kiss," *Helen of Troy,* 1911

✍ *Did men dislike sexual activity because they were so inept at it, or vice versa? This question would merit further study if such a thing were still possible.*

A guy and a girl are in the front seat of a car adjusting themselves after a quickie. The guy looks a little uncomfortable and says, "If I'd known you were a virgin, I would have taken more time."

The girl looks back at him and says, "If I'd known you weren't in such a hurry, I'd have taken off my panty hose."

•

Their lovemaking was fast and furious.
He was fast and she was furious.

—U.S. JOKES, 1980s

Most American men know more about the carburetor than the clitoris. —HENRY MILLER (1891–1980)

TEST YOUR KNOWLEDGE: MEN AND SEX

Why did God create man?
  Because a vibrator can't mow the lawn.

•

How can you tell if a man is a lousy lover?
  His inflatable woman has headaches.

•

What is a man's idea of foreplay?
  "You awake?"

•

What can you say to a man who's just had sex?
   Anything you like. He's asleep.

•

What is the correct technical term for when a woman has an orgasm during sex with a man?
   A miracle.

•

Why do men want to marry virgins?
   Because they can't stand criticism.

•

Having heard women like men with a sense of humor, what does
a man do to make his new girlfriend laugh?
   Shows her his privates.

•

Why are women bad at math?
   Because they are always told that this
   <———————————————————> equals ten inches.

•

What are the Three Ages of Man?
   Tri weekly; Try weekly; Try weakly.

•

How can you tell if you're having a super orgasm?
   Your boyfriend wakes up.

•

What is a perfect lover?

A guy with a nine-inch tongue who can breathe through his ears.

•

What food reminds women of their man's performance in bed?

Minute rice.

∾ *Why Is a Man like . . .*

. . . old age?

They both come too soon.

. . . a bottle of cheap sherry?

They're both lousy liquors.

. . . a cheap fireworks display?

One mediocre bang and the evening's over.

. . . a basketball player?

They both dribble when they're trying to score.

. . . a modern injection?

It's all over before you feel a thing.

. . . a straw hat?

Neither is felt.

. . . a hepatitis B injection?

A quick, short prick in the backside and it's finished.

. . . a mortgage?

The interest is unwelcome and the demands never end.

. . . a stamp?

One lick and they stick to you.

. . . a dog?

One stroke and they follow you everywhere.

. . . greasy hair?

Both tend to be lank, limp and lifeless when you want a bit of body.

. . . a commercial?

You can't believe a word either one says and they both last about thirty seconds.

. . . a snowstorm?

Because you don't know when he's coming, how many inches you'll get, or how long he'll stay.

. . . popcorn?

It'll satisfy you, but only for a little while.

. . . an old car?

They both need a lot of touching up before they can perform.

... a bad cello player?
They both sit and scratch their instrument instead of learning how to use it properly.

... a cake made with ordinary flour in the oven?
They both get very hot but still can't rise.

... a bus?
Neither comes when you want them to, then just as your patience has run out, they come all at once.

And What Is the Difference Between . . .

... hard and dark?
It stays dark all night long.

... a stud and an average man?
One's good for seconds, the other's good for seconds.

... a man and an egg?
In 7 minutes an egg can be hard; in 7 minutes a man will be soft.

... a 6-pack and lovemaking?
A man can make a 6-pack last more than ten minutes.

... a man and a hot fudge sundae?
A hot fudge sundae will satisfy a woman every time.
—U.S., British, Canadian and Australian jokes, 1990–93

SEX REDUX, OR, NO LAUGHING MATTER

> *Such unseemly jocularity began to dwindle once sapi-ents recognized the loathsome nature of concupiscence.*
>
> From self-knowledge thou wilt gain hatred of thine own fleshliness, and through hate thou wilt become a judge, and sit upon the seat of thy con-science, and pass judgment; and thou wilt not let a fault go without giving sentence on it.
>
> —St. Catherine of Siena, letter to
> Monna Alessa di Saracini, c. 1370

Sensuality, too, which used to show itself coarse, smiling, un-masked, and unmistakable, is now serious, analytic, and so burdened with a sense of its responsibilities that it passes muster half the time as a new type of asceticism.

> —Agnes Repplier, "Fiction in the Pulpit,"
> *Points of View,* 1891

The feminist movement is currently in a state of deep division over where to place sexuality within feminist theory and prac-tice. . . . As work is to Marxism, sexuality is to feminism.

Many women are currently embracing and defending a patriar-chally constructed notion of sex. . . . Women's advocacy of patriarchal sexual relations is a part of the phenomenon of identification with the oppressor. . . .

When women defend pornography and patriarchally con-structed sex . . . they are "timing" sexual abuse in the same manner as do some women in battering relationships. We do not need to define our liberation as an acceptance of the erotic inequality that character-izes the turn-on of the patriarchy.

—Wendy Stock, Ph.D., "Toward a Feminist
Praxis of Sexuality," 1990

In truth, the activity once known as sexual intercourse was nothing but . . .

. . . an assertion of mastery, one that announces [the man's] higher caste and proves it upon a victim who is expected to surrender, serve, and be satisfied.
—Kate Millett, *Sexual Politics,* 1970

Intercourse is the pure, sterile, formal expression of men's con-tempt for women. . . . [It is] a *literal* erosion of the [female] body's in-tegrity and its ability to function and survive . . . her insides are worn away over time, and she, possessed, becomes weak, depleted, usurped in all her physical and mental en-ergies and capacities by the one who has physically taken her over. . . . Perhaps incestuous rape is becoming a central paradigm for intercourse in our time. . . . Getting fucked and being owned are in-separably the same.

—Andrea Dworkin, *Intercourse,* 1987

It is no accident that the "missionary" position is the favored one in advanced patriarchy. The man is "on top" in bed just as he is in the economy and politics. The woman is pinned down, can hardly move, and has the least chance of having an orgasm. If marriage is legalized prostitution, then heterosexuality is socially approved rape.

— COLETTA REID, "Coming Out in the Women's Movement," c. 1974

Sex is the cross on which women are crucified. . . . Sex can only be adequately defined as universal rape.

— HODEE EDWARDS, "Rape Defines Sex," *Off Our Backs,* AUGUST–SEPTEMBER 1993

In the male system, women are sex, sex is the whore. . . . Men control the sexual and reproductive uses of women's bodies. The institutions of control include law, marriage, prostitution, pornography, health care, the economy, organized religion, and systematized physical aggression against women. . . . The metaphysics of male sexual domination is that women are whores. . . . One does not violate something by using it for what it is: neither rape nor prostitution is an abuse of the female because in both the female is fulfilling her natural function.

— ANDREA DWORKIN, *Pornography: Men Possessing Women,* 1981

What is sexual is what gives a man an erection. . . . If there is no inequality, no violation, no dominance, no force, there is no sexual arousal. —Catharine MacKinnon

❧ *One may wonder whether it wasn't excessively* submissive *for women (especially those who called themselves feminists) to allow the male response to define sex. But when men stalked the earth, they owned* everything.

Female sexuality still depends upon male demand, and male demand is more genital-centered and more specific than women's urge to express sensuality and tenderness. . . . The kind of sex that leaves women pregnant is not the kind that gives them the most pleasure, but it is the kind they usually get. . . . To accept contraception is to choose between two unacceptable alternatives, forced pregnancy or temporary infertility with a greater or lesser degree of present discomfort or malaise and unknown and unguessable long-term consequences.

—Germaine Greer, "The Backlash Myth" in *The New Republic,*
October 5, 1992

❧ QUESTION: *Wasn't the "sexual liberation" movement of the 1960s and 1970s good for women?*
ANSWER: *Absolutely not!*

Women's liberation has done more for men than it ever did for women. —Anon. (male), 1980

"Sexual liberation" is not the liberation of women, but the liberation of the female sex-object, which is now expected to orgasm (in response).

—Susanne Kappeler, *The Pornography of Representation,* 1986

Having an orgasm during intercourse is an adaptation of our bodies. Intercourse was never meant to stimulate women to orgasm.

—Shere Hite, *The Hite Report,* 1976

⟡ *Sex was never a private matter.*

Heterosexual sex for most people is in no way free of the power relations between men and women.

—Dierdre English and Barbara Ehrenreich, 1979 (and others)

The normative status of heterosexuality forces women to limit themselves sexually and emotionally to relationships with members of the caste that oppresses them. . . . Viewed in this light the straight norm is not really a sexual norm at all, but a powerful instrument in the perpetuation of the power relationship between the sexes.

—Purple September, a Dutch collective, c. 1972

⟡ *How liberating it was to learn that sex was nothing but a phallo-hegemonic ideology!*

Heterosexual Ideology

Ideological hegemony means that there is an ideology that exercises total control over the assumptions under which people live. . . . In terms of the oppression of women, heterosexuality is the ideology of male supremacy. . . .

Heterosexual hegemony insures that people think it natural that male and female form a life-long sexual/reproductive unit with the female belonging to the male. . . . Heterosexual hegemony insures that people can't even perceive that there could be other possibilities. . . .

If the ideology of heterosexuality can be attacked and exposed and an alternative ideology can be developed, I'm not sure how important it is that all women stop being heterosexual. . . . If you're going to have a baby, there is a role for heterosexuality. If we develop other ways to have babies, then what heterosexuality is becomes irrelevant.　MARGARET SMALL, "Lesbians and the

Class Position of Women," c. 1972

THE ILLUSION
CALLED LOVE

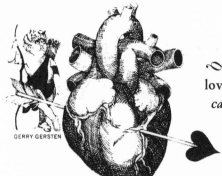

GERRY GERSTEN

✧ *What about the phenomenon called love between man and woman that one occasionally reads about? Was there ever such a thing, and if so, what was it?*

Love is a grave mental disease.
—PLATO (427?–347 B.C.)

This thing called love, there's none of it, you know, it's only fucking. That's all there is—just fucking.
—SAMUEL BECKETT (1906–1989)

You mustn't force sex to do the work of love or love to do the work of sex. —MARY McCARTHY

Don't threaten me with love, baby. (Let's just go walking in the rain.) —BILLIE HOLIDAY (1915–1959)

I am not a cold woman, Henry,
But I do not feel for you,
What I feel for the elephants and the miasmas,
And the general view.
—STEVIE SMITH, "Lady 'Rogue' Singleton," 1972

✧ *What used to be called "love" was only an unhealthy dramatization of the quintessentially male struggle for power.*

Given an Oppressor—the will for power—the natural response for its counterpart, the Oppressed . . . is Self-annihilation. . . . The most common female escape is the psychopathological condition of love. It is a euphoric state of fantasy in which the victim transforms her oppressor into her redeemer. . . . "Love" is the natural response of the victim to the rapist.

> —Ti-Grace Atkinson, "Radical Feminism," c. 1970

We love what we should scorn if we were wiser.

> —Marie de France, 12th century

Love, love, love—all the wretched cant of it, masking egotism, lust, masochism, fantasy under a mythology of sentimental postures, a welter of self-induced miseries and joys, blinding and masking the essential personalities in the frozen gestures of courtship, in the kissing and the dating and the desire, the compliments and the quarrels which vivify its barrenness.

> —Germaine Greer, *The Female Eunuch,* 1971

Those who thought they could live on love were merely courting starvation.

Love's a thin diet, nor will keep out a cold.

> —Aphra Behn, *The Lucky Chance,* 1686

Love says, mine. Love says, I could eat you up. Love says, stay as you are, be my own private thing, don't you dare have ideas I don't share. Love has just got to gobble the other, bones and all, crunch. I don't want to do that. I sure don't want it done to me! —MARGE PIERCY, *Braided Lives,* 1982

Love never dies of starvation, but often of indigestion.
  —NINON DE LENCLOS, 1660

Oh this man
what a meal he made of me
how he chewed and gobbled and sucked
in the end he spat me all out.
  —MICHELE ROBERTS, "Magnificat," 1970–80

◌ *Love was a terrible thing.*

Love was a terrible thing. You poisoned it and stabbed at it and knocked it down into the mud—well down—and it got up and staggered on, bleeding and muddy and awful. Like—like Rasputin.
  —JEAN RHYS, *Quartet,* 1928

Four be the things I am wiser to know:
Idleness, sorrow, a friend, and a foe.
Four be the things I'd be better without:
Love, curiosity, freckles, and doubt.
  —DOROTHY PARKER, "Inventory," 1927

◦ *Parker's four naive wishes were granted a mere generation later. Even freckles became passé when the sun (a well-known masculine symbol) became a thing to be shunned. But nothing became obsolete so quickly and absolutely as "romantic" love, once the Truth was revealed.*

What in the liberal view looks like love and romance looks a lot like hatred and torture to the feminist.

—CATHARINE MACKINNON, *Toward a Feminist Theory of the State*, 1989

With lovers like men, who needs torturers?
—SUSANNE KAPPELER, *The Pornography of Representation*, 1986

◦ *Strange as it may seem, before the Great Millennial Revolution people not only engaged in heterosexualism, they even wrote and spoke about it!*

PORNOGRAPHY—THE DEVIL'S WORKSHOP

⋄ *What was pornography? The phallocentric view:*

pornography, *n*. (Gr. *porne,* prostitute, and *graphein,* to write.) 1. originally, a description of prostitutes and their trade. 2. writings, pictures, etc. intended to arouse sexual desire. 3. the production of such writings, pictures, etc.

  —Webster's New Universal Unabridged Dictionary, 2nd ed., 1983

⋄ *Enlightened ideologists knew better.*

Pornography is propaganda against women.

•

Pornography is the theory, rape is the practice.

  —Feminist slogans, 1980s

Pornography is not about sex. It's about an imbalance of male-female power that allows and even requires sex to be used as a form of aggression. . . . But until we finally untangle sexuality and aggression, there will be more pornography and less erotica. There will be little murders in our beds—and very little love.

  —Gloria Steinem, *Outrageous Acts and Everyday Rebellions,* 1983

138

Pornography is, of course, masturbation material. It's used as sex. It therefore is sex. . . . Women being exposed, humiliated, violated, degraded, mutilated, dismembered, bound, gagged, tortured and killed . . . Men come doing this. This, too, is behavior. It is not a thought. It is not an argument. If you think it is, try arguing with an orgasm.

—Catharine MacKinnon, *Speech, Equality and Harm Conference,*
University of Chicago Law School, 1993

In [the work of de] Sade, the authentic equation is revealed: the power of the pornographer is the power of the rapist batterer is the power of the man.

—Andrea Dworkin, *Pornography,* 1987

❧ *Did the existence of erotic writing and pictures invariably lead to rape and murder? Of course it did!*

An FBI study of 36 sexual serial killers found that pornography was ranked highest of many sexual interests by an astonishing 81 percent.

—Jane Caputi and Diana E.H. Russell, "'Femicide': Speaking the Unspeakable," *Ms.,*
September–October 1990

⌘ *In light of these horrors, it became evident that some judicious controls were in order.*

If the pen is indeed mightier than the sword, should it not be subject to the same controls, licensing and non-proliferation treaties?
—MARY MCINTOSH, "Liberalism and the Contradictions of Sexual Politics," 1992

It is a civil rights issue when a group of citizens are being degraded. This is an issue where civil rights should supersede First Amendment rights.
—PATRICE SAYRE, president, Des Moines chapter of NOW, on the Indianapolis antipornography ordinance, 1984

⌘ *Censorship in the United States had a long and noble history. The Comstock Laws (1873) banned from the federal mails all publications of an "obscene" character, including any "lewd and lascivious" or "filthy" material, or anything with an "indecent or immoral purpose." This definition . . .*

. . . was broad enough to exclude discussion of birth control, marriage counseling, and abortion for years.
—WILLIAM PRESTON, historian, 1992

⌘ *This was highly prescient, since now that heterosexualism has gone the way of "men," the discussion of such matters is no longer an issue.*

ALL MEN ARE RAPISTS

࿄ *For "men," sex and violence were inextricably linked. A typical man asked:*

What well-made man, in a word, what man endowed with vigorous organs does not desire, in one fashion or in another, to molest his partner during his enjoyment of her?

—Marquis de Sade, *Philosophy in the Bedroom,* 1795

࿄ *It was clear to the discerning that all "men," if allowed to roam about the world unrestrained, are potential rapists.*

It appears that a large percentage of the male population has a propensity to rape.

—Diana E. H. Russell, "Pornography and Violence: What Does the New Research Say?," 1980

All men are rapists and that's all they are.

—Marilyn French, author of *The Women's Room,* 1983

࿄ *What political function did rape serve when "men" still controlled the world?*

Rape is a direct expression of sexual politics, an assertion of masculine norms, and a form of terrorism that preserves the gender status quo.

—Jane Caputi and Diana E. H. Russell, "'Femicide': Speaking the Unspeakable," *Ms.,* September–October 1990

Since you can't tell who has the potential for rape by simply looking, be on your guard with every man.

— ANDREA PARROT, *Acquaintance Rape and Sexual Assault Prevention Training Manual,* 1988

From prehistoric times to the present, rape has played a critical function. It is nothing more nor less than a conscious process of intimidation by which *all men* keep *all women* in a state of fear.

— ALISON JAGGAR, *Feminist Politics and Human Nature,* 1983

Cultural representation of glamorized degradation has created a situation among the young in which boys rape and girls get raped *as a normal course of events.*

— NAOMI WOLF, *The Beauty Myth,* 1991

Compare victims' reports of rape with women's reports of sex. They look a lot alike. . . . In this light, the major distinction between intercourse (normal) and rape (abnormal) is that the normal happens so often that one cannot get anyone to see anything wrong with it.

— CATHARINE MACKINNON, in *Ethics,* Vol. 99, No. 2, JANUARY 1989

❧ QUESTION: *Didn't the identification of normal sexual activity with the heinous crime of rape insult and trivialize the experience of the* real *victims of violent sexual assault?*
ANSWER: *Anyone who asks that question deserves to get raped! After all, when men still ran wild, rape was . . .*

. . . more common than left-handedness or heart attacks or alcoholism.
—Robin Warshaw, feminist writer, 1993

Men see rape as intercourse; feminists say much intercourse "is" rape . . . feminism stresses the indistinguishability of prostitution, marriage, and sexual harassment.
—Catharine MacKinnon, *Feminism Unmodified,* 1987

Acquaintance rape spans a spectrum of incidents and behaviors ranging from crimes legally defined as rape to verbal harassment and inappropriate innuendo.
—Swarthmore College
training guide, 1985

❧ *Yes, inappropriate innuendo! You got a problem with that?*

Many [people] distinguish between "real rape" and what they insist are "gray areas.". . . Those who make the distinction are, in effect, collaborators. . . .

144

Sexual assaults flourish in a climate of "gray areas." So long as the myth of "real" rape survives, rapists will thrive. And we will all pay for their evil entertainment.

—Alice Vachss, "All Rape is 'Real' Rape," Op-Ed page,
The New York Times, August 11, 1993

◦◦◦ "Men" who did not wish to be considered rapists (if any) learned to weigh with utmost care their words and deeds—and both "men" and sapients honed their communication skills to perfection.

The absence of a no doesn't mean yes.

—Kelly Gifford, Rutgers University Women's Support and
Resource Center, 1993

Silence throughout an entire physical encounter with someone is not explicit consent.   —Director, Columbia University's date-rape
education program, 1992

Sexual intercourse . . . without the expressed consent of the person [shall be defined in campus disciplinary proceedings as rape].

—Harvard University Date Rape Task Force, 1992

◦◦◦ A court upheld the "expressed consent" standard in a case where a pair of petting teenagers went too far, and the boy immediately ceased his activity when the girl requested that he stop.

Any act of sexual penetration engaged in by the defendant without the affirmative and freely-given permission of the victim to the specific act of penetration [meets the definition of force required by law, and there was] no burden on the alleged victim to have expressed non-consent or to have denied permission.

—New Jersey Supreme Court, 1991, upholding a rape conviction
where no force was used

✣ *Antioch, the progressive college, broke new ground in this ambiguous terrain.*

"Consent" [is] the act of willingly and verbally agreeing to engage in specific sexual contact or conduct. . . . Verbal consent should be obtained with each new level of physical and/or sexual contact/conduct in any given interaction, regardless of who initiates it. Asking, "Do you want to have sex with me?" is not enough. The request for consent must be specific to each act.

—Antioch College Date Rape Code, 1993

✣ *The most advanced thinkers questioned whether a woman's consent was even a meaningful concept.*

So long as women are powerless relative to men, viewing a "yes" as a sign of true consent is misguided. . . . Many women who say yes . . . would say no if they could. . . . Women's silence sometimes is the product not of passion and desire but of pressure and fear.

—Susan Estrich, *Real Rape,* 1987

Consent as ideology cannot be distinguished from habitual acquiescence, assent, silent dissent, submission, or even enforced submission. Unless refusal of consent or withdrawal of consent are real possibilities, we can no longer speak of "consent" in any genuine sense.

—CAROL PATEMAN, "Women and Consent,"
Political Theory, MAY 1980

Was it rape if one enjoyed it? If one didn't? Could one decide after the event that, on reflection, the activity was not what one thought it was at all?

"Yes," I answered you last night;
"No," this morning, sir, I say.
Colours seen by candle-light
Will not look the same by day.

—ELIZABETH BARRETT BROWNING, "The Lady's Yes," 1844

I am not suggesting that it's rape unless she has an orgasm—though I doubt if any woman who had an orgasm Saturday night called it date rape Sunday morning.

—ELLEN GOODMAN, "Sexual Liberation and the Pleasure Principle,"
The Boston Globe, OCTOBER 30, 1993

A man exploits a woman every time he uses her body for sexual pleasure while he is unwilling to accept the full burden of paternity. . . . That is to say single men (and frequently married men) exploit women almost every time they make love. [The woman] may consent fully, knowledgeably, enthusiastically to her exploitation. That does not change the nature of the transaction.

—MAGGIE GALLAGHER, *Enemies of Eros,* 1990

✑ *At one time, prospective victims were occasionally saved by divine intervention.*

A Thwarted Rapist

Sister Hroswitha of Gandersheim, the first medieval playwright, dramatized the story of three Christian girls who were commanded by the Emperor Diocletian to abjure their faith. When they refused, he handed them over to General Dulcetius for execution. Dulcetius imprisoned them in a room next to the kitchen, intending to return later to ravish them. But that night, he lost his way. Befuddled, he caressed the cookware, while the girls watched through a crack in the wall:

"The fool is out of his mind; he fancies he has got hold of us!" reported one of the girls. "Now he presses the kettle to his heart, now he clasps the pots and pans and presses his lips to them. . . . His face, his hands, his clothes are all black with soot; the soot that clings to him makes him look like he has just come straight from Hell."

"Very fitting that he should be so in body," remarks one of her companions, "since the Devil has possession of his mind."

—HROSWITHA OF GANDERSHEIM, *Dulcetius,* c. A.D. 975.

❧ *Advice to students on avoiding the tragedy of unwanted sexual advances:*

In order that no such thing may ever happen to thee, be on thy guard: let not thy misfortune be such as to enter into any private conversation, with monk or layman. For if I were to know or hear it, even if I were much farther away than I am, I would give thee such a discipline that it would stay in thy memory all thy whole life; never mind who may be by.

—St. Catherine of Siena (1347–1380),
letter to Sister Eugenia, her niece

Sit not with another in a place that is too narrow, read not out of the same book; let not your eagerness to see anything induce you to place your head close to another person's.

—Eliza Farrar, *The Young Lady's Friend*, 1837

When a man kisses a woman against her will, she is fully entitled to bite off his nose if she so pleases.

—Legal ruling, London, England, 1837, denying damages to Thomas Saverland, victim of nose-biting

SEXUAL HARASSMENT—A GLOBAL OUTRAGE

➣ *What was sexual harassment, when it still existed? From a typical university code:*

Sexual harassment . . . may involve . . . suggestive comments, jokes, or remarks . . . suggestive looks or gestures . . . and physical attack, including rape. . . .

If you are uncomfortable and believe that you are a victim of sexual harassment, talk to someone who will help you sort out your feelings and label the behavior. . . .

Victims are affected in many ways, all of them negative. . . . Victims need to know that their feelings are real and they should not be told to ignore their reactions or to forget what has happened.

—University of Rhode Island pamphlet, "Be Free! Sexual
Harassment Oppresses All of Us," 1993

～ *Sexual harassment may include:*

. . . comments, jokes, gestures or looks . . .
—"Hostile Hallways: American Association of University Women
Survey on Sexual Harassment in American Schools," 1993

. . . inappropriate laughter . . .
—Sarah Lawrence College, University of Connecticut (and others)

. . . staring or leering with sexual overtones and . . . spreading sexual gossip.   —Amherst Pelham Regional High Schools, 1991

[It can be] as subtle as a look [and often consists of] callous insensitivity to the experience of women.
—University of Minnesota sexual harassment code, 1984

～ *A punishable offense?*

A male student makes remarks in a class like "Women just aren't as good in this field as men," thus creating a hostile learning atmosphere for female classmates.

—University of Michigan "Policy on Discrimination and
Discriminatory Harassment," 1991

Freedom of speech should belong mainly to the powerless rather than those in power.... The powerless are all members of "outsider" groups, like blacks and women, no matter how affluent and influential the individual.

—Mari Matsuda, critical race theorist at Stanford Law School,
quoted in *The New York Times,* June 29, 1990

◦ *Are words as powerful as deeds?*

More than three hundred [U.S.] institutions of higher learning punish speech either in specific speech codes or as a part of their overall rules for conduct.

—Michael Olivas, associate dean for research,
University of Houston Law Center, 1992

◦ *Are thoughts as powerful as words?*

Warning

Lately several women have reported being stared at by men while they are studying here at Memorial [Library]. Because of the various descriptions they have given us, we know that more than one man is doing this. Please do not let yourself be victimized.

If you become aware that someone is staring at you, *do not tolerate this behavior*. Come down to the Circulation Desk and report the problem. Or pick up the red phone near the elevator. In either case, please be willing to stay to talk to the police. . . .

Be alert. Help us protect your right to study in peace!

—Notice posted in April 1993, in Memorial Library,
University of Wisconsin at Madison

⌘ *Over the years, some callous persons objected to the exquisite levels of sensitivity required to avoid causing offense.*

Imaginary evils are incurable.

—Marie von Ebner-Eschenbach, *Aphorisms*, 1905

CURB YOUR ANIMAL INSTINCT

CONTROLA TU INSTINTO ANIMAL

⌘ *The answer to such cynics:*

A lustful glance can feel as threatening as a violent grab. . . . Some gestures are more heinous than others, but they're all intimidating. . . .

Most men have participated in street abuse. . . . There's a commonly held belief that because women don't respond to abuse, that they love it or it's just not affecting them.

—Susan Hadleigh-West, filmmaker, 1993. (Her *War Zone* documents street abuse by men: 112 incidents in 2 days.)

~ *According to the U.S. Department of Labor:*

The EEOC [Equal Employment Opportunity Commission] recognizes that sexual conduct may be private and unacknowledged, with no eyewitnesses. Therefore, in appropriate cases, it may make a finding of harassment based solely on the credibility of the victim's allegation. . . .

An employer . . . may be responsible for the acts of its agents and supervisory employees, regardless of whether the specific acts complained of were forbidden and regardless of whether the employer knew of their occurrence. . . . Lack of knowledge about such harassment does not necessarily protect the employer from liability. . . . An employer may also be responsible for sexual harassment by clients or customers.

—U.S. DEPARTMENT OF LABOR, Leaflet 55, "A Working Woman's
Guide to Her Job Rights," 1992

~ *These liberating concepts rapidly moved out into the wider world.*

Now that the premise of actionable "hostile and offensive" work places has been accepted, there is no reason not to press on with the concept of a "hostile and offensive world"!

—SHEILA KUEHL, attorney, at Speech, Equality and Harm
Conference, Chicago, 1993

✑ A song for anti–sexual harassment activists:

We're angry. The brainless bird who
    tangles with *us*
    has gummed his last mush.
In fact, the coot who even heckles
    is being daringly rash.
So look to your nests, you reclaimed
    eagles—
    whatever you lay, we'll squash!

         —Chorus of Women in Aristophanes, *Lysistrata,* 411 b.c.

A bully is not unreasonable—he is persuaded only by threats.

         —Marie de France, 12th century

WALKING THE WORLD IN FEAR

✑ In the old days, women had to decide whether to walk the world in fear...

At one point [women's] fears were confined to dark, secluded alleys. Now women must worry about crowded offices, local restaurants, and comfortable homes. For women, there is no longer any place they can call "secure."

         —U.S. Senate staff report, "The Violence Against
         Women Act of 1993"

All the world's a cage.   —JEANNE PHILLIPS

✑ *... or in terror.*

The murders of women by husbands, lovers, fathers, acquaintances, and strangers are not the products of some inexplicable deviance. Murder is simply the most extreme form of sexist terrorism....

Femicide is the ultimate end of a continuum of terror that includes rape, torture, mutilation, sexual slavery ... child sexual abuse, physical and emotional battery; sexual harassment; genital mutilations ... forced heterosexuality, forced sterilization, forced motherhood . . . cosmetic surgery and other mutilations in the name of beautification....

The vast majority of serial killers are white men and most of their victims are women....

If all femicides were recognized as such and accurately counted . . . if the patriarchal home were seen as the inescapable prison it so frequently becomes, if pornography and gorenography were recognized as hate literature, then this culture might have to acknowledge that we live in the midst of a reign of sexist terror comparable in magnitude, intensity, and intent to the persecution, torture, and annihilation of women as witches from the 14th to the 17th centuries in Europe.

    —JANE CAPUTI AND DIANA E. H. RUSSELL, "'Femicide': Speaking the
              Unspeakable," *Ms.,* SEPTEMBER–OCTOBER 1990

✑ *For women, the world was an incredibly threatening place—*

especially with all those white men running loose.

What happened in Montreal [a mass murder of women by a white man] may forever stand out in our minds as the ultimate assault against women. Yet it's the monotonous quality of the violence—the threats, slaps, kicks, slugs, knifings, rapes, and murders—which is the backdrop of our daily lives. . . . It just never seems to stop.

—Rita Jensen, "A Day in the Life," *Ms.,* September–October 1990

A white man grabbed an African-American woman off the street, assaulted her, directed both racist and sexist hate speech at her, threw lighter fluid on her genitals and set her on fire. Horrible, horrible crime, but an increasingly commonplace crime.

—Mari Matsuda, critical race theorist, University of Chicago Law School, Speech, Equality and Harm Conference, 1993

White men make up only 8 percent of the world population. I find that an encouraging fact.

—Deborah Rhode, Stanford law professor, 1993

POLITICALLY CORRECT SEX

•❧• *As the patriarchy waned, the few sapients who still engaged in heterosexualism devised more egalitarian ways to go about it.*

During my shows, I like to call men up from the audience. I like to see men in the position of women. To see their faces when I tear off

their shirts, make them lie down on the stage. Now it's the man who's on the bottom! I, a woman, undress the man! Sometimes I take off their belts and whip them. *Sí!* The way they often hit women. I believe that the next time they're with their girls they'll be sweeter, more romantic, because now they know how girls feel. Also, it's fun for the girls in the audience— they get an eyeball taco. Which is to say, they get a good look at the boy I've left without his clothes.

—Gloria Trevi, Mexican pop star, interview in
The New Yorker, April 26, 1993

A thorough overhaul of desire is clearly on the feminist agenda: the fantasy that we are overwhelmed by Rhett Butler should be traded in for one in which we seize state power and re-educate him.

—Professor Sandra Lee Bartky, *Femininity and Domination: Studies in the Phenomenology of Oppression,* 1990

⟋◌⟍ *During the late phalloheteropatriarchy, anonymous manifestos championing "correct sex" began appearing in college and public library books. From the Danbury [Connecticut] Public Library:*

Female-dominant Sex: A Call to Action

Objective: Eliminate the perception of male sexual superiority over women.

Strategy: A woman can gain sexual power over a man by consistently refusing to participate in conventional sex (which is "boring") and agreeing to have sex with him only if she is dominant.

Method: Each sexual experience must include the performance of a fantasy scenario in which she . . . sexually humiliates him by forcing him to strip naked in front of her at gunpoint; renders him physically helpless by handcuffing his wrists and tying his ankles to the bedposts so he is spread-eagled on his back; ties a short cord snugly around his scrotum and penis for use as a tourniquet; convincingly describes to him, in great detail, how she will castrate him and cut off his penis at the peak of his sexual pleasure; forces and excites his erection; applies a condom and has sexual intercourse with him while holding a dull knife to his scrotum, constantly teasing him about his castration at the moment of ejaculation; allows him to ejaculate but then forces him to sincerely beg her not to castrate him; forces him to agree to be her sex slave for the rest of his life if she does not castrate him; handcuffs his hands behind his back, attaches a leash to his tourniquet, and forces him to kneel in front of her nude, reclining body, progressively licking her breasts, her vulva (until she climaxes) and her feet, until she is convinced his submission is complete.

The woman must play this fantasy as an exciting and enjoyable game.... The man's observation of her pleasure, and his own pleasure during intercourse, will keep him coming back for more.... Gradually he will accept the idea that his body is her sexual plaything, and will enjoy being psychologically abused by her during sex.... The woman uses and abuses the male body in the ways which give her the greatest pleasure, just as men have used and abused the female body for their pleasure since the dawn of humanity.

Discussion: A woman enjoys the castration fantasy because it instantly avenges all the sexual domination ever committed by men over women.... It is also an exciting, erotic experience for a man.... As this fantasy is repeated again and again, his sole source of sexual pleasure becomes the pleasure of the sexual victim—a pleasure he has always thought to be reserved only for women. With each repeti-

tion of this fantasy, a man's
mental association of
sexual pleasure with
domination over women
becomes weaker. Event-
ually, this result of his socialization as a man will
be just a faded memory.

Caveat: The castra-
tion fantasy is a necessary
means for the achievement
of sexual equality in our society.
It must always remain only a fantasy, however. Actual sexual mutilation of men is counterproductive. . . . Men have been rendered permanently impotent by sexual tortures, such as crushing, piercing and
applying extreme heat or electric shocks to their testicles. Many men
have died during these sexual tortures.

Please: Network! Send copies of this sheet to all of your sexually
active female acquaintances. Also place copies in feminine-interest
books at your public library. This works. Find the "right kind" of
man and do it! . . . NOW!

— ANON., "Female-Dominant Sex," 1992

❧ *Such idealistic sentiments presumed that men were educable, even
though ten thousand years of experience have shown that they are not.*

There's nothing so stubborn as a man when you want him to do
something.   — JEAN GIRAUDOUX, *The Madwoman of Chaillot*, 1945

Sometimes I think if there was a third sex men wouldn't get so much as a glance from me.　　—Amanda Vail, *Love Me Little,* 1958

✧ *So what was a poor sapient to do?*

SEX WITHOUT MEN

✧ *Sapients in ever-increasing numbers began to discover that sex without men had a great deal to recommend it.*

What Lesbianism Offers You

Lesbianism... offers you the freedom to be yourself.... It offers escape from the silly, stupid, harmful games that men and women play, having the nerve to call them "relationships." It offers change.... A free, strong self cannot live in the muck that men have made.... You will discover the thousand subtle ways that heterosexuality destroyed your true power; you will discover how male supremacy destroys all women.... You will build communities with other women from all classes and races.... You will share what you have with others and they with you. You will revolt against the whole filthy world that tried to cover you and your beauty under a ton of male supremacist slime. That is what Lesbianism offers you.

　　—Rita Mae Brown, "The Shape of Things To Come," c. 1970

For a woman to be a lesbian in a male-supremacist, capitalist, misogynist, racist, homophobic, imperialist culture, such as that of North America, is an act of resistance.

  —CHERYL CLARKE, "Lesbianism: An Act of Resistance," c. 1980

∾ *Why straight women were sellouts:*

To say that "Everybody needs love and I could care less if a woman is fucking a man" is to say "Any oppressed person needs some payoff to make them preserve their oppression. I could care less if a woman is oppressed, and I could care less if that oppression makes her gang up with that pig to fuck me over." . . .

Any woman relating to a man cannot be a feminist. Women who give love and energy to men . . . will wish to remain in a society that says men are better than women, and they'll join their boyfriends in trying to do us in.

It's really sad that every man holds a woman in front of him to cushion reality and be his shield. . . . Well, I'm not going to try to take on all those women. . . . I personally am going to keep my distance from men and straight women. Maybe we can run around behind and stab that pig in the back. Any woman hanging out in front to protect him would then have the choice of joining us or letting him fall on top of her.

  —BARBARA SOLOMON, "Taking the Bullshit by the Horns," *The*
     Furies, MARCH–APRIL 1972

A short note about bisexuality. You can't have your cake and eat it too. . . .

  —RITA MAE BROWN, "The Shape of Things To Come," c. 1970

➣ *Some seekers of exotic sexual experience began looking to space aliens, as in the following example:*

The shower door opened and Pauldor stood naked, sort of.... Terri's eyes went to his groin. Her face brightened. He was not only well-hung, but he had almost a dozen erections over his chest and stomach. Each one just as red and rigid as the one in his groin.

He got in and embraced her. The projections attached themselves to her with squishing suction pops. The last one slid gingerly in where it should. Terri yelped with pleasure and pain as the suction grew. Then she moved like she'd never done before. She gave it all she had....

She was there. She howled, thankful she was not at home where Earl said everyone in the surrounding trailers could hear her. Paul gave an equally loud, but more pained sound, and the erections popped off. He stared down at his groin for a moment, seeming not to believe what he saw, then collapsed onto the shower floor.

—ROBERTA LANNES, "Saving the World at the New Moon Motel," 1990

➣ *How about sex with no physical contact whatsoever! Consider these reports of spiritual ecstasy:*

My body is in long torment, my soul in high delight, for she has seen and embraced her Beloved.... As He draws her to Himself, she gives herself to Him. She cannot hold back and so He takes her to Himself. Gladly would she speak but dares not. She is engulfed. . . . He gives her a brief respite that she may long for

Him. . . . He looks at her and
draws her to Him with a
greeting the body may not
know.

—Mechtild of Magdeburg

(1210–1297)

The angel held a long
golden dart in his hands.
From time to time he
plunged it into my heart and
forced it into my entrails.
When he withdrew the dart,
it was as if he were going to tear out my entrails, and it left me all in-
flamed with love divine. . . . I am certain that the pain penetrated my
deepest entrails and it seemed as if they were torn when my spiritual
spouse withdrew the arrow with which he had penetrated them.

—St. Theresa of Avila

🌣 *Margery Kempe was the author of the first autobiography in English.*
God revealed to her that He would be to her like a great lord who is hus-
band to a poor woman, saying:

"Daughter . . . when thou art in thy bed, take Me to thee as thy
wedded husband. . . . Boldly take Me in the arms of thy soul and kiss
My mouth, My head, and My feet, as sweetly as thou wilt." . . .

God bestowed on [Margery] a physical token which endured
about sixteen years, and it increased ever more and more, and that

was a flame of fire, wondrous hot and delectable, and right comfortable, not wasting but ever increasing, of love; for though the weather was never so cold she felt the heat burning in her breast and at her heart. —MARGERY KEMPE, *The Book of Margery Kempe,* 1436

In the end, nothing beats no sex at all.

If sex is a war, I am a conscientious objector: I will not play.
—MARGE PIERCY, *Braided Lives,* 1982

Purity is the ability to contemplate defilement.
—SIMONE WEIL, *Gravity and Grace,* 1974

Beware of fleshly lusts, which war against the soul.
—SYLVESTER GRAHAM, M.D. (1802–1851), vegetarian, sexologist,
inventor of the Graham cracker

ALL SEX MUST STOP

The ultimate insight, by a late-20th-century writing collective:

A Statement by Women Against Sex:
All Sex Must Stop
Before Male Supremacy Will Be Defeated

Since we believe that the practice of sexuality politically subordinates women we believe that the entire practice must be dismantled.... Though we realize that many women ... have had self-described affirmative sexual experiences, we believe that this was in spite of and not because the experiences were sexual....

We believe that homosexuality, pedophilia, lesbianism, bisexuality, transsexuality, transvestism, sadomasochism, nonfeminist celibacy, and autoeroticism have the same malevolent relationship to conceptual and empirical male force as does heterosexuality.... There is no way out of the practice of sexuality except *out*.... *We know of no exception to male supremacist sex*.... We therefore name intercourse, penetration, and all other sex acts as integral parts of the male gender construction which is sex; and we criticize them as oppressive to women. We name orgasm as the epistemological mark of the sexual, and we therefore criticize it too as oppressive to women....

Historically, sex acts have included rape, marital rape, footbinding, fellatio, intercourse, autoeroticism, forced sex, objectification, child rape, incest, battery, anal intercourse, use and production of pornography, pimping and the use/abuse of prostitutes, cunnilingus, sexual harassment, torture, mutilation, and murder—especially by dismemberment, strangulation, and stabbing....

A sex act can be operationally defined as an act which, if a woman does not choose it, a male *qua* male would find it genitally arousing to force her.... It is politics made flesh.... Any act informed by a practice ... which did not subordinate women—would literally not be a sex act. More succinctly: *if it doesn't subordinate women, it's not sex*....

The patriarchy attempts to reach *within* women to fuck/construct us from the inside out. This attempt assumes many forms, such as sex "education" and sex advice. . . .

If we can teach pigeons to play Ping-Pong, incarnating in them desires they never thought they had, perhaps we can teach ourselves to prefer a nonsexualized woman-identification to the desire for subordination and for self-annihilation that is the required content and social paradigm of our sexuality. . . .

Sex has to stop before male supremacy will be defeated.

— WOMEN AGAINST SEX (A Southern Women's Writing Collective),
"Sex Resistance in Heterosexual Arrangements," 1987

To the Barricades!

✧ *Clearly a global transformation was in order. Let us explore the ground of the Great Millennial Revolution and hear the rousing calls to arms that transformed our world into the paradise on earth that it is today.*

WHO IS THE ENEMY?

✧ *The first step to victory is to identify the enemy.*

Men are the enemy.
—Germaine Greer, *The Female Eunuch,* 1970, and elsewhere

Men are . . . the enemies and the Oppressors of women.
—"The Feminists" Manifesto, 1968

To have a good enemy, choose a friend: he knows where to strike.
—Diane de Poitiers (1499–1566)

It is hard to fight an enemy who has outposts in your head.
—Sally Kempton, "Cutting Loose," in *Esquire,* July 1970

ᐳ *On the other hand, maybe "men" were not really the enemy, but merely codependent victims of the patriarchy.*

Men weren't really the enemy—they were fellow victims suffering from an outmoded masculine mystique that made them feel unnecessarily inadequate when there were no bears to kill.
—Betty Friedan, in *The Christian Science Monitor,* 1974

ᐳ *Maybe the family was the enemy.*

The family is the most violent group in society, with the exception of the police and the military.
—Dr. Joyce Brothers, quoting University of Rhode Island
sociologist Richard Gelles, 1993

ᐳ *Or maybe the govern(person)t was the enemy.*

We've never been in a democracy; we've always been in a phallocracy!　　—Françoise Parturier, *Open Letter to Men,* 1968

This is a government of, by, and for a bunch of *assholes.* Men in government butt-fuck whoever gets in the way of their war games, their head trips, and their death trips. Life is all about getting

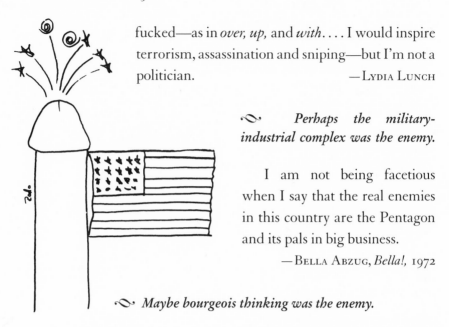

fucked—as in *over, up,* and *with.* . . . I would inspire terrorism, assassination and sniping—but I'm not a politician.
—LYDIA LUNCH

◌ *Perhaps the military-industrial complex was the enemy.*

I am not being facetious when I say that the real enemies in this country are the Pentagon and its pals in big business.
—BELLA ABZUG, *Bella!,* 1972

◌ *Maybe bourgeois thinking was the enemy.*

It is the precise juncture of bourgeois and male interest which constitutes the cornerstone of women's experience and corresponding oppression.
—DR. SUSAN S. M. EDWARDS, *Policing "Domestic" Violence,* 1989

God Almighty made the women and the Rockefeller gang of thieves made the ladies.
—MOTHER JONES (1843–1930)

◌ *Or maybe Judeo-Christian civilization was the enemy.*

The prevailing opinion, that woman was created for man, may have taken its rise from Moses's poetical story; yet, as very few . . . who have bestowed any serious thought on the subject, ever supposed that Eve was, literally speaking, one of Adam's ribs, the deduction must be allowed to fall . . . or, only be so far admitted as it proves that man, from the remotest antiquity, found it convenient to exert his strength to subjugate his companion, and his invention to show that she ought to have her neck bent under the yoke, because the whole creation was only created for his convenience or pleasure. . . .

— MARY WOLLSTONECRAFT, *A Vindication of the Rights of Women,* 1792

The ethos of Judeo-Christian culture is dominated by the Most Unholy Trinity: Rape, Genocide, and War. It is rapism which spawns racism. It is gynocide which spawns genocide, for sexism (rapism) is fundamental socialization to objectify "the other."

— MARY DALY, professor of theology at Boston College, *Beyond God the Father,* 1973

MEN AND CIVILIZATION

✧ *Even though women throughout herstory attempted to be a civilizing force, it was obvious that man alone created what was once known as civilization—in his own vile image.*

Men created civilization in the image of a perpetual erection: a *pregnant* phallus.

— PHYLLIS CHESLER, *About Men,* 1978

It's a man's world, and you men can have it.

— KATHERINE ANNE PORTER

174

 ❧ *Before we stopped him, the male beast was intent upon the destruction of Mother Earth herself!*

Slowly the wasters and despoilers are impoverishing our land, our nature, and our beauty, so that there will not be one beach, one hill, one lane, one meadow, one forest free from the debris of man and the stigma of his improvidence. —MARY MANNES, 1962

I saw that animals, trees, seas, and indeed the entire beautiful planet Earth were being dismembered by phallocrats.

—MARY DALY, *Outercourse*, 1992

 ❧ *The male mode of thinking, modeled on the penis (verticalism), was to blame for this appalling state of affairs.*

The vertical system . . . represents exact thinking or decisiveness, or mastery of something, or being able to make an argument. . . . [The vertical psyche] is triggered by words such as "excellence," "accomplishment," "success," and "achievement" . . . [ideas which] represent a hidden ethos that has made a few white males dangerous to themselves and to the rest of us, especially in a nuclear age.

—PEGGY McINTOSH, associate director, Center for Research on Women, Wellesley College, 1993

∾ *What was once naively considered "great art" exemplified the phallohegemonic obsession.*

Michelangelo was a pornographer.   —CAMILLE PAGLIA

∾ *The music of Beethoven represented gynocidal rapism at its worst.*

As if the thrusting impulse characteristic of tonality and the aggression characteristic of first themes were not enough, Beethoven's symphonies add two other dimensions to the history of style: assaultive pelvic pounding . . . and sexual violence. The point of recapitulation in the first movement of the Ninth is one of the most horrifying moments in music, as the carefully prepared cadence is frustrated, damming up energy which finally explodes in the throttling, murderous rage of a rapist incapable of attaining release.
—PROFESSOR SUSAN MCCLARY, feminist musicologist,
"Getting Down Off the Beanstalk," in *Minnesota
Composers' Forum Newsletter,* JANUARY 1987

∾ *Landscape photography, another "art" invented by men, provided a perfect example of the pornographic mind at work:*

The parallels between pornography and landscape photography are illuminating and deeply disturbing to anyone concerned about the environment. Like a centerfold model, the towering peak or other monumental landform is posed in an intimate setting. Provocative lighting—dawn, alpenglow, or storm light—is preferred. . . .
It might be argued that since the primary complaint against

pornography is the trivialization of women as sex objects, then land-scape photography cannot be pornographic because landforms *are* objects and the content of the images is not sexual. What this argu-ment truly reveals, however, is the depth of our cultural sickness. . . . The Grand Tetons and the Grand Canyon are stereo-typed objects of idealized, romanticized desire in our cultural psyche. The glamorization of these particular protrusions and cleavages in the erogenous zones of our collective imagination has damaged both them and us. . . . We are collectively seduced by the rectangular storm-light portrait of the bosom of the Grand Tetons, with its crafted illusion of intimacy, overlooking its total detachment from the surrounding high plains, where herds of antelope, trapped on public lands by grazing-allotment fences, starve to death and wait to be buried by drifting snow.

— José Knighton, "Eco-Porn and the Manipulation of
Desire," in *Wild Earth,* Spring 1993

✆ *Not to mention the assaults of "science"!*

If we put it in the most blatant feminist terms used today, we'd talk about marital rape, the husband as scientist forcing nature to his wishes. . . . Is it not as illuminating and honest to refer to Newton's laws as "Newton's rape manual" as it is to call them "Newton's me-chanics"?

— Sandra G. Harding, professor of philosophy and director of
women's studies, University of Delaware,
The Science Question in Feminism, 1986

∽ *Knowledge itself, as construed in those days, was nothing but rape-murder.*

Mind was male, Nature was female, and knowledge was created as an act of aggression.

—Elizabeth Fee, in *Feminist Approaches to Science,* 1986

All naming is already murder.
—Jacques Lacan (1901–1981)

Feminist analysis begins with the principle that objective reality is a myth. . . . Male and female perceptions of value are not shared, and are perhaps not even perceptible to each other.

—Ann Scales, feminist legal scholar, in the *Yale Law School Review,* c. 1990

∽ *Our foremothers had a daunting task before them.*

[Women] are confronted virtually with the problem of *reinventing* the world of knowledge, of thought, of symbols and images. Not of course by repudiating everything that has been done, but by subjecting it to exacting scrutiny and criticism from the position of women as subject . . . or knower.

—Dorothy E. Smith, "Ideological Structure and How Women Are Excluded," c. 1980

‿ *This was not easy, considering that men exercised iron control over all language.*

MOTHER TONGUE-TIED: State or condition of any language in the mouths of its female speakers; female linguistic plight/pain of trying to get men to listen to, not just hear, what she is saying. *See:* Enguish.

•

ENGUISH: Male-dominated and -dictated language of women in the patriarchy; state of female linguistic pain at being forced to suppress women's words and meanings.

—KATE MUSGRAVE, *Womb with Views,* 1989

Overcoming the man-made pseudopresences requires continuing Leaping through Realms of Reality beyond the banal boundaries set by foolish deadfellows. This implies nothing less than Dis-covering and Re-weaving strands of the X-factor, that ever convergence of Strange, Variable, and Diverse Qualities that characterize Questing women.

—MARY DALY, *Webster's First New Intergalactic Wickedary,* 1987

ALL MEN ARE VIOLENT

‿ *"Men," having created "civilization" in their own image, exercising the suicidal impulse so characteristic of their species, set immediately about destroying it.*

Men have now gone so far in the mastery of natural forces that with their help they could easily exterminate one another to the last man. They know this, hence a large part of their current unrest, their unhappiness, their mood of anxiety.

—Sigmund Freud, *Civilization and Its Discontents,* 1929

I am a feminist because I feel endangered, psychically and physically, by this society and because I believe that the women's movement is saying that we have come to an edge of history when men—insofar as they are embodiments of the patriarchal idea— have become dangerous to children and other living things, themselves included.

—Adrienne Rich, *On Lies, Secrets and Silence,* 1979

If you're not a feminist, you're a masochist.

—Gloria Steinem

[Weapons of war are] phallic toys . . . cannons and aeroplanes and all those things, and men need phallic toys and women do not. Now

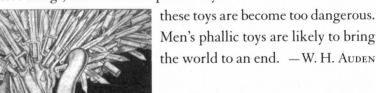

these toys are become too dangerous. Men's phallic toys are likely to bring the world to an end. —W. H. Auden

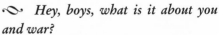 *Hey, boys, what is it about you and war?*

Hey, boys, what is it about you and war, huh? In my Club Scud days in Tel Aviv during the Gulf War, I remember seeing a study about how

men and women respond sexually to war. Women who are living in battle zones turn solitary and introspective, completely repulsed by the idea of coupling, while men basically find war to be a big turn-on, the ultimate aftershave.

—Kathy McManus, "Letter from Liberia," in *Esquire,* August 1993

Did "men" pursue war solely as a means of recreation?

I realize that were I a man, I would be at the battlefront fighting amidst bullets and explosives, instead of sitting serenely at my desk.

—Kieko Yamamuro, untitled essay, 1895
(during the Russo-Japanese War)

Although "men" may have covered their aggression with the fiction that they were fighting to "protect" women and children from the depredations of other "men," it was always clear that if there were no "men," there would be no war.

I loathe with all my heart the first of men who slew
A human fellow-being when the earth was new.
My spirit shrinks from him who for primeval raids
Made sharp the world's first arrow, honed the first of blades.
For sure that soul rose up from Hades black as sin
That first conceived the thought of murdering to win.
He was by Furies nurtured who with savage lust
First ground gunpowder, first a bullet cast.
He waged his war against all humankind and won,
Oh, he has marred all Nature with his baneful gun. . . .
Masked lunacy, thy foot is round and weighs like lead,
And where it treads, a sea of blood is shed!

—Anna Luisa Karsch, "Anger at War,
When It Lasted Too Long," 1764

❧ *All male violence is founded on violence against women.*

All the seeds of social abominations such as savagery, barbarism, and civilization have as their sole pivot the subjection of women.

—CHARLES FOURIER, "Design for Utopia," 1971

❧ *Did* all men *hate* all women?

Male hostility to women is a constant; all men hate all women some of the time; some men hate all women all of the time; some men hate some women all of the time. Unfortunately, women cannot bring themselves to hate men, possibly because they carry them in their wombs from time to time.

—GERMAINE GREER, "The Backlash Myth," in
The New Republic, OCTOBER 5, 1992

Maybe a man was nothing but a man, which is what Baby Suggs always said. They encouraged you to put some of your weight in their hands and soon as you felt how light and lovely that was, they studied your scars and tribulations, after which they did what he had done: ran her children out and tore up the house. . . .

"A man ain't nothing but a man," said Baby Suggs. "But a son? Well now, that's *somebody*."   —Toni Morrison, *Beloved*, 1978

➥ *If all "men" were hostile and violent, what, if anything, was a* **good man?**

In all men is evil sleeping; the good man is he who will not awaken it, in himself or in other men.

—Mary Renault, *The Praise Singer*, 1978

ALL WOMEN ARE VIRTUOUS

➥ *The spiritual superiority of women is a gift directly from God.*

The Lord gives these [spiritual] favors far more to women than to men; I have heard the saintly Fray Peter of Alcantara say that, and I have observed it myself. He would say that women made much more progress on this road than men, and gave excellent reasons for this, which there is no point in my repeating here, all in favor of women.   —St. Theresa of Avila

Women do not kill anyone, wound or torture them; they do not plot or carry out treacherous acts, they are not arsonists, nor do they disinherit anyone, administer poison, steal gold or silver, trick people out of their possessions or lawful inheritance through fraudulent contracts, nor harm kingdoms, duchies, or empires. . . . For woman's nature is noble, very compassionate, timid, and timorous. She is humble, gentle, self-effacing, and full of charity, loveable, devout, and quietly modest. She fears war, is innocent and pious; when annoyed, her anger is quick to subside; she cannot bear to witness cruelty or suffering, and in a word, this is the female character, which clearly stems from her nature.

—CHRISTINE DE PIZAN, "The Letter of the
God of Love" (poem), 1399

Where did your Christ come from? From God and a woman! Man had nothing to do with Him.

—SOJOURNER TRUTH, speech, 1851

The spirit of the valley never dies. It is called the Mysterious
  Female.
The gate of the Mysterious Female is the source of heaven and
  earth. It lives forever. Enter without effort.

—LAO-TSE, *Tao Teh Ching,* C. 500 B.C.

The Eternal Feminine draws us upward!

—JOHANN WOLFGANG VON GOETHE, *Faust,* 1833

The woman is life, and the man is the servant of life.

—JOSEPH CAMPBELL, 1988, explaining why women are in the center
of a tribal dance, why they control the dance, and
why the men dance around the women

Woman is the creator and fosterer of life; man has been the mechanizer and destroyer of life. . . . The maternalizing influences of being a mother . . . made the female the more humane of the sexes.

—ASHLEY MONTAGU, *The Natural Superiority of Women,* 1952

Woman must lead the efforts in education for peace awareness, because only she can . . . go back to her womb, her roots, her natural rhythms, her inner search for harmony and peace.

—PETRA KELLY, *Fighting for Hope,* 1984

And I know, in the depth of my being and in all my knowledge of history and humanity, I know women will struggle for a social order of peace, equality and joy.

—JOAN KELLY, historian, on the eve of her death, 1982

✑ *A premature prediction:*

I'm confident our great nation will have a woman President before the year 1900. And I am equally confident that having a lady in
the President's office will make our country a far better place to live.

— ABRAHAM LINCOLN, journal entry, 1861

✑ *Virtue herself is a lady.*

Virtue herself, by name and fashion
Is a lady. . . . You seldom see the ladies
Using bows and flaming arrows on their men—
Men are often deceivers, girls hardly ever. . . .

— OVID, *The Art of Love,* c. A.D. 5

Everything I learn reinforces my conviction that the only correc-
tive to social inequality, cruelty and callousness is to be found in values
which, if we cannot call them female, can be called sororal. They are
the opposite of competitiveness, acquisitiveness and domination, and
may be summed up by the word "co-operation." In the world of sis-
terhood, all deserve care and attention. . . . Perfect love casteth out fear.
The only perfect love to be found on earth is not sexual love, which is
riddled with hostility and insecurity, but the wordless commitment of
families, which takes as its model mother-love. This is not to say that
fathers have no place, for father-love, with its driving for self-
improvement and discipline, is also essential to survival, but that un-
corrected father-love . . . is a way to annihilation.

— GERMAINE GREER, Introduction to
The Madwoman's Underclothes, 1986

୰ *A devout monk and poet, apprehending these truths, prayed that God would . . .*

Annul in me my manhood, Lord, and make
Me woman-sexed and weak
If by that total transformation
I might know Thee more.
What is the worth of my own sex
That the bold possessive instinct
Should but shoulder Thee aside?
What uselessness is housled in my loins,
To drive, drive the rampant pride of life,
When what is needful is a hushed
    quiescence?
"The soul is feminine to God,"
And hangs on impregnation,
Fertile influxing Grace. But how achieve
The elemental lapse of that repose,
That watchful, all-abiding silence of the soul,
In which the Lover enters to His own,
Yielding Himself to her, and her alone?
How may a man assume that hiddenness of heart
Being male, all masculine and male,
Blunt with male hunger? Make me then
Girl-hearted, virgin-souled, woman-docile, maiden-meek;
Cancel in me the rude compulsive tide
That like an angry river surges through,
Flouts off Thy soft lip-touches, froth-blinds

The soul-gaze from its very great delight,
Out-bawls the rare celestial melody.
Restless I churn. The use of sex is union,
Union alone. Here it but cleaves,
Makes man the futile ape of God, all ape
And no bride, usurps the energizing role, inverts;
And in that wrenched inversion caught
Draws off the needer from his never-ending need, diverts
The seeker from the Sought.

—BROTHER ANTONINUS, O.P., 1957

ALL WOMEN ARE VICTIMS

∽ *Women's superior virtue and spiritual simplicity led to their being relentlessly victimized by the predatory sex.*

Women are doormats and have been,
    The years these mats applaud—
They keep the men from going in
    With muddy feet to God.

         —MARY CAROLYN DAVIES, "Doormats," c. 1925

The history of mankind is the history of repeated injuries and usurpations practiced on the part of man toward woman.

         —SENECA FALLS DECLARATION, 1848

Oppressed, degraded, enslaved,—must our unfortunate sex for ever submit to sacrifice their right, their pleasures, their *will,* at the altar of public opinion?   —MARIA EDGEWORTH, *Angelina,* c. 1799

To be a woman is to feel your wings droop.
    —ST. THERESA OF AVILA, when her confessor forced her to destroy
         her translation of the Song of Solomon because it was
         unsuitable for a woman to have done it

Feminist consciousness is consciousness of *victimization* . . . to come to see oneself as a victim.
    —PROFESSOR SANDRA LEE BARTKY, *Femininity and Domination:*
         Studies in the Phenomenology of Oppression, 1990

Ninety-five percent of women's experiences are about being a victim. Or about being an underdog, or having to survive . . . women didn't go to Vietnam and blow things up. They are not Rambo.
    —JODIE FOSTER, interview in *The New*
    York Times Magazine, JANUARY 6, 1991

Womanhood is a mass pain of unspoken depth.

> —MARIANNE WILLIAMSON, *A Woman's Worth,* 1993

The king has been very good to me. He promoted me from a simple maid to be a marchioness. Then he raised me to be a queen. Now he will raise me to be a martyr.

> —ANNE BOLEYN, before her execution, 1536

Behind almost every woman you ever heard of stands a man who let her down. —NAOMI BLIVIN

☙ Nobody can deny that Victims occupy a loftier rung on the moral hierarchy than do Oppressors.

Possessed, as are all the fair daughters of Eve, of an hereditary propensity, transmitted to them undiminished through succeeding generations, to be "soon moved with the slightest touch of blame"; very little precept and practice will confirm them in the habit, and instruct them in all the maxims, of self-justification.

Candid pupil, you will readily accede to a first and sentimental axiom—that a lady can do no wrong.

> —MARIA EDGEWORTH, *An Essay on the Noble*
> *Science of Self-Justification,* 1787

As any psychologist will tell you, the worst thing you can possibly do to a woman is to deprive her of a grievance. —BEVERLY NICHOLS

Women and elephants never forget.

> —DOROTHY PARKER, "Ballad of Unfortunate
> Mammals," *Death and Taxes,* 1931

If a woman says she's been sexually assaulted, then she has been.
— TAKE BACK THE NIGHT, in *New York* magazine, MARCH 8, 1993

Women should be supported regardless of proof.
— ANITA HILL, in campus lectures

If the person feels hurt, then something wrong happened.
— VIRGINIA MACKAY-SMITH, Harvard Date Rape Task Force, 1993

To question any victim is hideously immoral.
— ROSEANNE ARNOLD, *Playboy* interview, JUNE 1993

EQUALITY . . .

∾   *Mary Wollstonecraft mistakenly urged women to renounce the superior moral status victimhood confers by cultivating strength.*

I wish to persuade women to endeavor to acquire strength, both of mind and body, and to convince them that soft phrases, susceptibility of heart, delicacy of sentiment, and refinement of taste, are almost synonymous with epithets of weakness and that those beings who are only objects of pity . . . will soon become objects of contempt.

Dismissing, then, those pretty feminine phrases, which the men condescendingly use to soften our slavish dependence, and despising that weak elegancy of mind, exquisite sensibility, and sweet docility of manners, supposed to be the sexual characteristics of the weaker vessel, I wish to show that elegance is inferior to virtue, that the first object of laudable ambition is to obtain a character as a human being, regardless of the distinction of sex. . . .

Men have superior strength of body, but were it not for the mistaken notions of beauty, women would acquire sufficient [strength] to enable them to earn their own subsistence, the true definition of independence.

— MARY WOLLSTONECRAFT, *Vindication of the Rights of Women,* 1792

∾ *Others also promulgated the pernicious doctrine of equality.*

Genius has no sex! — GERMAINE DE STAËL, c. 1810

A lion's cubs are lions all, male and female alike.
— RUSTAVELI, *The Knight in Panther's Skin,* on the accession of
Tamara Queen of Georgia, c. A.D. 1200

I can't change my sex. But you can change your policy.
— HELEN KIRKPATRICK, on being told a newspaper didn't have
women on its foreign-affairs staff, 1940

No one can make you
feel inferior without your
consent.
— ELEANOR ROOSEVELT,
in *Catholic Digest,* 1960

Are we not all
immortal beings?
Is not each one re-
sponsible for him-
self and herself?
— LYDIA MARIA
CHILD, abolitionist,
letter from New
York, 1860

Equal pay for equal work!   — FEMINIST SLOGAN, 1970s

Now free women must join in the human world of work and
creation on an equal footing and be everywhere in art, science, business, politics etc. . . . However, to lay claim, in this battle, to female
ethics, female criticism, female knowledge . . . is to set up a new female ghetto. (Male chauvinists should be delighted by this move.)
— IRIS MURDOCH, letter to Christina Sommers, 1990

There is more difference within the sexes than between them.
— IVY COMPTON-BURNETT (1884–1969)

The main difference between men and women is that men are lunatics and women are idiots.   —REBECCA WEST

Women in general are as fit for the offices of state, as those who most commonly fill them. All women are not born with great capacities any more than the men; but balance the account, and it will not, at least, poise against us.   —ANON., *Female Rights Vindicated,* 1758

❧ *When Golda Meir became Israel's Minister for Foreign Affairs, a reporter asked her how it felt to be a female foreign minister. She replied:*

I don't know, I've never been a male Foreign Minister.
                                        —GOLDA MEIR, 1956

❧ *Indira Gandhi, on being asked a similar question:*

As Prime Minister, I am not a woman. I am a human being. . . . Being a woman has neither helped nor hindered me. During the struggle for independence, nobody was concerned about my being beaten up or shot at or anything. Nobody said: "This is a woman and we won't shoot." It would be unfair if, later on, this question were to crop up.   —INDIRA GANDHI, 1975

❧ *The longest-serving 20th-century prime minister of a nation with a long herstory of powerful female rulers:*

The feminists have become far too strident and have done damage to the cause of women by making us out to be something we're not. You get on because you have the right talents. . . . I don't notice that I'm a woman. I regard myself as the Prime Minister.

—MARGARET THATCHER, 1978, 1980

. . . IS AN ILLUSION

❧ *And a dangerous one, at that.*

Women who want to be equal to men lack imagination.

—TIMOTHY LEARY

Flattery is when a woman demands equal rights. —ANON.

Equal rights for the sexes will be achieved when mediocre women occupy high positions. —FRANÇOISE GIROUD

Women are not men's equals in anything except responsibility. We are not their inferiors, either, or even their superiors. We are quite simply different races.

—PHYLLIS McGINLEY, "The Honor of Being a Woman," *The Province of the Heart,* 1959

The goal has grown from balancing, mainstreaming and integration (essentially addition) to transformation (radical paradigm shifts).

—PROFESSOR JOHNNELLA BUTLER, University of Washington, on the future of women's studies, 1993

The time has come to valorize woman's ideas at the expense of those of men. . . . In particular, it is the artist's task to give the greatest priority to everything that comes from the feminine system of the world.

—ANDRÉ BRETON,
Arcane 17, 1947

THE FATHERS OF THE SISTERS

᪣ *The Revolutionary Sisters may not have had any brothers, but they did have fathers.*

Monogamy does by no means enter history as a reconciliation of man and wife, and still less as the highest form of marriage. On the contrary, it enters as the subjugation of one sex by the other, as the proclamation of an antagonism between the sexes unknown in all preceding history. . . . The first class antagonism appearing in history coincides with the development of the antagonism of man and wife in monogamy, and the first class oppression with that of the female by the male sex.

—FRIEDRICH ENGELS, *Origin of the Family,*
Private Property, and the State, 1884

⌒ *Marx prescribed the perceptions necessary for large-scale revolution:*

A class must be formed which has radical chains, a class *in* civil society which is not a class *of* civil society, a class which is the dissolution of all classes. . . . For one class to represent the whole of society, another class must concentrate in itself all the evils of society. . . . For one class to be the liberating class *par excellence,* it is essential that another class should be openly the oppressing class.
—KARL MARX, *Criticism of Hegel's "Philosophy of Right,"* 1844

⌒ *Marx's daughters developed these theories with exquisite sensitivity to herstorical necessity.*

The protection of property rights and patriarchal privilege . . . will not yield without a struggle, and it will be the job of the state under socialism to see that these interests are suppressed and eliminated even if this runs counter to the expressed will of the people.
—PAULA ROTHENBERG, Marxist feminist
scholar, in *Socialist Visions,* 1993

⌒ *Some benighted souls failed to see themselves as oppressed. This delusion is called Denial, and it is death to liberation movements, since anyone who denies being oppressed is automatically colluding with the Oppressor. Resistance includes:*

Thinking that our man is the exception. . . .

Thinking that individual solutions are possible. . . .

Thinking that women's liberation is therapy. . . .

Thinking that some women are smart and some women are dumb. . . .

Thinking that only institutions oppress women . . . for institutions are only a tool of the oppressor. . . .

Thinking that male supremacy is only a psychological privilege with "ego" benefits as opposed to a class privilege with sexual and economic benefits. The former implies a considerable amount of individual variation among men. . . .

—IRENE PESLIKIS, "Resistances to Consciousness," 1969

⌒ *Women within the radical movements of the 1960s, finding themselves consigned to mimeography and coffee-making while the brothers retained all revolutionary glamour and publicity for themselves, formed their own alliances. From the Women's Liberation Caucus of the Youth International Party (YIPPIE!):*

When in the course of the progressive dialectic of history it becomes necessary for people oppressed by caste to off the nuclear family which stabilizes the capitalist, imperialist, military complex economy . . . a decent respect for the opinions of our sisters in struggle, compel [*sic*] us to assume the responsibility of the vanguard. The Women's Liberation Caucus within the Youth International Party, being through a rigorous analysis of the thoughts of Mao, Susan B. Anthony, Che, Lenin, and Groucho, considers itself bound by the historic necessity of becoming the vanguard party of the progressive women's revolution because we fly higher.

> — SCREWEE! (Society Condemning the Rape and Exploitation of Women Etc. Etc.), "An Exegesis On Women's Liberation," c. 1967

∾ The Yippie!s were revolutionary pranksters. One of their most successful demonstrations, for example, consisted of tossing dollar bills from the balcony of the New York Stock Exchange onto the trading floor. The stock market screeched to a halt while brokers who routinely deal in millions scrambled round the floor after the greenbacks. But most manifesto writers were deadly serious.

We take the woman's side in everything.

We ask not if something is "reformist," "radical," "revolutionary," or "moral." We ask: Is it good for women or bad for women? . . .

We define the best interests of women as the best interests of the poorest, most insulted, most despised, most abused woman on earth. . . . She is . . . what we all really are in the eyes of men . . . : ugly, dumb . . . bitch, nag, hag, whore, fucking and breeding machine, mother of us all. . . . When her beauty and knowledge is revealed and seen, the new day will be at hand. . . .

We regard our feelings as our most important source of political understanding.　—NEW YORK RADICAL WOMEN, "Principles," c. 1968

∾ *Another inspiring and original example:*

I. After centuries of individual and preliminary political struggle, women are uniting to achieve their final liberation from male supremacy. . . .

II. Women are an oppressed class. Our oppression is total, affecting every facet of our lives. . . . The conflicts between individual men and women are *political* conflicts that can only be solved collectively.

III. We identify the agents of our oppression as men. . . .

IV. Attempts have been made to shift the burden of responsibility to institutions. . . . Institutions . . . are merely tools of the oppressor. . . .

We also reject the idea that women consent to or are to blame for their own oppression. . . . We do not need to change ourselves, but to change men.

The most slanderous evasion of all is that women can oppress men. . . .

The time for individual skirmishes has passed. This time we are going all the way. —REDSTOCKINGS MANIFESTO, C. 1968

WOMEN AND REVOLUTION

∾ *The earliest female revolutionary in literature was the Athenian Lysistrata. Under her leadership the women of the warring city-states of ancient Greece united in refusing sexual favors to men until the men agreed to renounce war and disarm. Lysistrata's ingenious plan:*

We can force our husbands to negotiate Peace,
Ladies, by exercising steadfast Self-Control—
By total Abstinence . . . from SEX!

∾ *The oath Lysistrata administered to the women of Greece:*

I will withhold all rights of access or of entrance
From every husband, lover, or casual acquaintance
Who moves in my direction in erection.
I will create, imperforate in cloistered chastity,
A newer, more glamorous, supremely seductive me
And fire my husband's desire with my molten allure—
But remain, to his panting advances, icily pure.
If he should force me to share the connubial couch,
I refuse to return his stroke with the teeniest twitch.
I will not lift my slippers to touch the thatch
Or submit sloping prone in a hangdog crouch.
     If I this oath maintain,
         may I drink this glorious wine.
     But if I slip or falter,
         let me drink water. AMEN!

•∿• *Lysistrata calls the troops into battle:*

> . . . Onward, you ladies from hell!
> Forward, you market militia, you battle-hardened
> bargain hunters, old sales campaigners, grocery
> grenadiers, veterans never bested by an overcharge!
> You troops of the breadline, doughgirls—
> >   INTO THE FRAY!
> Show them no mercy!
> >   Push! Jostle! Shove!
> Call them nasty names! (Don't be ladylike.)

•∿• *The attack was successful and the enemy routed, leaving only a dazed old Commissioner muttering to himself, "A sorry day for the Forces." Lysistrata answered:*

> Of course. What did you expect? We're not slaves;
> we're freeborn Women, and when we're scorned, we're
> full of fury. Never Underestimate the Power of a Woman.
> >   —ARISTOPHANES, *Lysistrata,* 411 B.C.

•∿• *Herstory is full of female revolutionaries, although their exploits were not always reported in the media. Some 18th-century press reports:*

A number of women . . . proceeded to Gosden wind-mill, where, abusing the miller for having served them with brown flour, they seized on the cloth with which he was then dressing meal . . . and cut it into a thousand pieces; threatening at the same time to serve all similar utensils he might in future attempt to use in the same manner.

The amazonian leader of the petticoated cavalcade afterwards regaled her associates with a guinea's worth of liquor at the Crab Tree public house.

—ANON., 18th-century news report

Taunton, Somersetshire, June 25. Several hundred women . . . assembled in this town, in a tumultuous manner, and proceeded to a large weir [dam] . . . near a set of grist-mills call'd the Town-mills, when the women went briskly to work demolishing it, and that so as to prevent any corn being ground at the mills. The men all the while stood lookers on, giving the women many huzzas and commendations for their dexterity in the work. Their reason for it was a dislike they had to the manager of the mills, whom they charge with sending flour to other parts, whereby they apprehend corn was advanced to a higher price than otherwise it would have been.

—ANON., *Gentleman's Magazine,* 1743

Last Saturday a female mob assembled in the market place at Hereford, upon information that one of the badgers had offered to buy grain above the market price; and, after seizing the badger, and beating him in a very severe manner, they broke all the windows in his house.

—ANON., *London Chronicle,* 1757

❧ A 20th-century revolutionary commented:

The argument of the broken pane of glass is the most valuable argument in modern politics.

—EMMELINE PANKHURST, 1913

❧ Such job actions may be considered all the more stunning in light of sapients' superior gentleness and pacifism.

Yet in order to preserve the highest ideals, many were prepared to make the ultimate sacrifice. Herstory records the stirring words of many famous fighting queens.

I am fighting as an ordinary person for my lost freedom, my bruised body and my outraged daughters. . . . Consider how many of you are fighting—and why. Then you will win this battle, or perish. That is what I, a woman, plan to do! Let the men live in slavery if they will.

—QUEEN BOADICEA OF BRITAIN, to her troops, before their last stand against the Romans, A.D. 60

Thou askest me to surrender . . . as if thou wert ignorant that Queen Cleopatra chose rather to perish than to survive her dignity.

—QUEEN ZENOBIA OF PALMYRA, to the Roman Emperor Aurelian, A.D. 271

There is only one thing to be done, let us fight the Monster, let us beat the Monster down, and then we can talk of worries!
—QUEEN LOUISE OF PRUSSIA, on Napoleon, 1805

⌁ *Women have always been superior revolutionaries.*

In rebellion alone, woman is at ease, stamping out both prejudices and sufferings; all intellectual women will sooner or later rise in rebellion.
—LOUISE MICHEL, 1890

Intellect does not attain its full force unless it attacks power.
—GERMAINE DE STAËL, *The Influence of Literature Upon Society,* 1800

Men represent the deliberative and democratic element in life. Woman represents the despotic.
—G. K. CHESTERTON, "Woman," *All Things Considered,* 1908

Women and Revolution! What tragic, unsung epics of courage lie silent in the world's history!
—YANG PING, "Fragments from a Lost Diary," c. 1970

Women are natural guerrillas. Scheming, we nestle into the enemy's bed, avoiding open warfare, watching the options, playing the odds.
—SALLY KEMPTON

There are two kinds of women: those who want power in the world, and those who want power in bed.
—JACQUELINE KENNEDY ONASSIS

The revolution begins at home.
—CHERRIE MORAGA AND GLORIA ANZALDUA, *This Bridge Called My Back,* 1983

~ *Sapients have always had a special relationship to politics.*

In politics, if you want anything said, ask a man; if you want anything done, ask a woman. —MARGARET THATCHER

Roosters crow, hens deliver. —FEMINIST SLOGAN

The man reaps, the woman builds. —LEBANESE PROVERB

The reason there are so few female politicians is that it is too much trouble to put makeup on two faces. —MAUREEN MURPHY

There are far too many men in politics and not enough elsewhere. —HERMIONE GINGOLD, *How to Grow Old Disgracefully,* 1988

The divine right of husbands, like the divine right of kings, may, it is hoped, in this enlightened age, be contested without danger.
—MARY WOLLSTONECRAFT, *A Vindication of the Rights of Women,* 1792

A FRIENDLY WARNING

❧ *A friendly warning from Abigail Adams, wife of one U.S. president and mother of another. Her husband was at the First Continental Congress in Philadelphia, drafting the new Constitution, when she wrote to him:*

In the new code of laws which I suppose it will be necessary for you to make, I desire you would remember the ladies and be more generous and favorable to them than your ancestors. Do not put such unlimited power into the hands of the husbands. Remember, all men would be tyrants if they could. If particular care and attention is not paid to the ladies, we are determined to foment a rebellion, and will not hold ourselves bound by any laws in which we have no voice or representation.

That your sex are naturally tyrannical is a truth so thoroughly established as to admit of no dispute; but such of you as wish to be happy willingly give up the harsh title of master for the more tender and endearing one of friend. Why, then, not put it out of the power of the vicious and the lawless to use us with cruelty and indignity with impunity. Men of sense in all ages abhor those customs which treat us only as the vassals of your sex.

— Abigail Adams, letter to John Adams, March 31, 1776

❧ *John's amused reply:*

As to your extraordinary code of laws, I cannot but laugh. We have been told that our struggle has loosened the bonds of government everywhere; that children and apprentices were disobedient;

that schools and colleges were grown turbulent; that Indians slighted their guardians, and Negroes grew insolent to their masters. But your letter was the first intimation that another tribe, more numerous and powerful than all the rest, were grown discontented.

—JOHN ADAMS, letter to Abigail Adams, APRIL 14, 1776

꙳ *Abigail's serene answer:*

I cannot say that I think you are very generous to the ladies; for, whilst you are proclaiming peace and good-will to men, emancipating all nations, you insist upon retaining an absolute power over wives. But you must remember that arbitrary power is like most other things which are very hard, very liable to be broken; and, notwithstanding all your wise laws and maxims, we have it in our power, not only to free ourselves, but to subdue our masters, and without violence, throw both your natural and legal authority at our feet;—"Charm by accepting, by submitting sway, Yet have our humor most when we obey."

—ABIGAIL ADAMS, letter to John Adams, MAY 7, 1776

꙳ *John's response to Abigail's mildly worded threat is unrecorded, perhaps because he had no idea what she was talking about.*

A hundred years later, nothing had changed.

If the very next Congress refuses women all the legitimate results of citi-

zenship . . . we shall proceed to call another convention expressly to frame a new constitution and to erect a new government. . . . We mean treason; we mean secession, and on a thousand times grander scale than was that of the South. We are plotting a revolution; we will overthrow this bogus Republic and plant a government of righteousness in its stead.
  —Victoria Woodhull, to the National Woman Suffrage Association convention, 1872

❧ *And a hundred years later, things **still** had not changed.*

The vote, I thought, means nothing to women. We should be armed.
  —Edna O'Brien

STAY UP AND FIGHT!

❧ *Selected calls to arms:*

Never go to bed mad. Stay up and fight.
 —Phyllis Diller, *Phyllis Diller's Housekeeping Hints,* 1966

Obtain power, then, by all means; power is the law of man; make it yours.
  —Maria Edgeworth, *An Essay on the Noble Science of Self-Justification,* 1787

No real social change has ever come about without a revolution.
  —Emma Goldman, title essay, *Anarchism,* 1910

It is better to die on your feet than to live on your knees.

—Dolores Ibarruri (La Pasionaria), speech
in Paris, September 3, 1936

There was one of two things I had a *right* to, liberty, or death; if I could not have one, I would have the other; for no man should take me alive. —Harriet Tubman (1820–1913)

Don't liberate me—I'll do it myself!

•

Revolution must happen inside us before it is achieved in reality. . . . A cop sleeps inside each of us—it is necessary to kill him! —Anon., graffiti, May 1968

Let vengeance rule, not pity. I shall let the dogs tear you to pieces.

—Caterina Sforza, Countess of Forlì, to her enemies, 1490

The beast in me's eager and fit for a brawl.
Just rile me a bit and she'll kick down the wall.
You'll bawl to your friends that you've no balls at all.

—Chorus of Women in Aristophanes, *Lysistrata,* 411 B.C.

✎ *Revolution offered side benefits:*

Social activism is not a question of courage or bravery for me. There's no cheaper way to have fun, is there?

—Florynce Kennedy

Revolution is the festival of the oppressed.

—GERMAINE GREER, *The Female Eunuch,* 1971

❧ *The victory of women promised to be a victory for men as well.*

Can man be free if woman be a slave?

—PERCY BYSSHE SHELLEY (1792–1822)

Every time a new nation, America or Russia for instance, advances toward civilization, the human race perfects itself; every time an inferior class emerges from enslavement and degradation, the human race again perfects itself.

—GERMAINE DE STAËL, *The Influence of
Literature upon Society,* 1800

What we owe men is some freedom from their part in a murderous game in which they kick each other to death with one foot, bracing themselves on our various comfortable places with the other.

—GRACE PALEY

❧ *When the annihilation of "men" as a class was first proposed, a few hu(person)s may have objected that the program resembled the male paradigm of oppression. The answer to such cynics: Why shouldn't it?*

Oppressed people are frequently very oppressive when first liberated. And why wouldn't they be? They know the two best positions. Somebody's foot on their neck or their foot on somebody's neck.

—FLORYNCE KENNEDY, "Institutionalized
Oppression vs. the Female," 1970

Of all the nasty outcomes predicted for women's liberation . . .
none was more alarming, from a feminist point of view, than the sug-
gestion that women would eventually become just like men.
— BARBARA EHRENREICH, "The Real and Ever-Widening
Gender Gap," *Esquire,* JUNE 1984

Some of us are becoming the men we wanted to marry.
— GLORIA STEINEM, in *Ms.,* JULY–AUGUST 1982

༄ *Women were well advised not to hold back.*

The thing women have to learn is that nobody gives you power.
You just take it.   — ROSEANNE ARNOLD

YES, injured Woman! rise, assert thy right!
Woman! too long degraded, scorned, oppressed;
O born to rule in partial Law's despite,
Resume by native empire o'er the breast!

Go forth arrayed in panoply divine,
That angel pureness which admits no stain;
Go, bid proud Man his boasted rule resign
And kiss the golden scepter of thy reign. . . .

Try all that wit and art suggest to bend
Of thy imperial foe the stubborn knee;

Make treacherous Man thy subject, not thy friend;
Thou mayst command, but never canst be free.

Awe the licentious and restrain the rude;
Soften the sullen, clear the cloudy brow:
Be, more than princes' gifts, thy favours sued;—
She hazards all, who will the least allow.

— ANNA LAETITIA BARBAULD, *The Rights of Woman,* 1795

꙰ *No one can make a revolution all by herself.*

It is the easiest thing in the world to say every broad for herself—saying it and acting that way is one thing that's kept some of us behind the eight ball where we've been living for a hundred years.

—BILLIE HOLIDAY

If the first woman God ever made was strong enough to turn the world upside down all alone, these women together ought to be able to turn it back, and get it right side up again.

—SOJOURNER TRUTH (1797–1883)

꙰ *"Men" can never claim that the inevitable descended without warning.*

Streams of the sacred rivers flow uphill;
Tradition, order, all things are reversed:
    Deceit is *men*'s device now,
    Men's oaths are gods' dishonour.
Legend will now reverse our reputation;
A time comes when the female sex is honoured;
    That old discordant slander
    Shall no more hold us subject.

—CHORUS in Euripides, *Medea,* 431 B.C.

Double, bubble, war and rubble,

When you mess with women, you'll be in trouble. . . .

We curse your empire to make it fall—

When you take on one of us, you take on us all!

       —W.I.T.C.H., "Conspiracy Against Women," c. 1970

A World without Men

⌖ Second-millennium visionaries accurately prophesied that in the utopia that was rapidly approaching, there would be No Men at All!

HEAVEN ON EARTH

Can you imagine a world without men? No crime and lots of happy fat women. —Nicole Hollander ("Sylvia")

If they could put one man on the moon, why can't they put them all? —Unknown

Safety for Women? Try Removing Men.
—Ellen Goodman, article title, *Santa Barbara News-Press,* January 9, 1990

I'm Calamity Jane. Get to hell out of here and let me alone!

—Calamity Jane (Martha Jane
Cannary, 1852–1903)

⤳ *The Goddess Isis herself, through her oracles, predicted that the ultimate sapient triumph would occur near the year 2000 of the patriarchal era.*

When the Tenth Generation goes down to Hades
There comes a Woman's great power . . .
And then the whole wide world under a woman's hand . . .
Even Rome, the delicate gilded voluptuous maiden,
Will be at a mistress' stern command.

—Ptolemaic Creed of Isis, *The Sybilline Books,* c. 50 B.C.

⤳ *The extinction of the male was part of the natural evolutionary process.*

The penis is obviously going the way of the vermiform appendix.

—Jill Johnston

⤳ *By the end of the patriarchal aberration it was commonly observed that men died earlier than women at every age from all major causes of death, including heart disease, cancer, alcoholism, accidents and violence. Overall, they committed suicide at a rate four times that of women. This was obviously part of their genetic programming. But there were spiritual as well as physical reasons why the race of men was destined to wither away.*

Men's spirituality is very badly mangled. . . . Men don't have intuition or sensitivity. . . . Women have total mind. Men's minds are not true. . . . We must learn about men and their archetypes in order to put them back in their place—they are an aberration and out of control. . . . Men won't exist for much longer.

—J. HIGGINBOTTOM AND M. ROY, in *Feminist Action 1,* 1984

In evolutionary terms, females are more advanced than males. Women are more human than men.

—ASHLEY MONTAGU, *The Natural Superiority of Women,* 1952

You can think of maleness as a type of birth defect.

—DR. STEPHEN WACHTEL, Memorial Sloan-Kettering Cancer Center (and others)

THE REDUNDANT MALE

By the end of the phallocratic era, science and technology (ironically, male inventions: another example of the male penchant for suicide) were hastening to render the male obsolete.

One of the anthropological pleasures of the 1990's will be watching how men cope with a new role—that of the redundant male. New technology will wipe out their traditional advantages at work, favouring as it does female skills based on dexterity, not strength. An influx of skilled mature women into the workforce will erode the self-protective isolation on which men have built their authority. More than a quarter of live births are outside marriage, marginalising the father in the family; he will no longer automatically be the only, nor even the main, breadwinner. As a final nail in the male coffin by the mid-1990's it will be simple for single women who want children to become pregnant through artificial insemination. This is already available to a limited number of women in specialised private clinics, and could well pave the way to a viable alternative for women to the old-fashioned male-female parental relationship.

—JANE MCLOUGHLIN, *The Democratic Revolution,* 1991

A man is so in the way in the house!
—ELIZABETH GASKELL, *Cranford,* 1853

The fact is that men need women more than women need men; and so, aware of this fact, man has sought to keep woman dependent upon him economically as the only method open to him of making himself necessary to her. —ELIZABETH GOULD DAVIS, *The First Sex,* 1971

222

Man's role is uncertain, undefined, and perhaps unnecessary. By a great effort man has hit upon a method of compensating himself for his basic inferiority.

—Margaret Mead

❧ *Many agreed all along that in the ideal world fathers might well be dispensed with.*

Fathers should be neither seen nor heard. That is the only proper basis for family life.

—Oscar Wilde

I phoned my dad to tell him I had stopped smoking. He called me a quitter.

—Steven Pearl

One father is more than a hundred schoolmasters.

—George Herbert (1593–1633)

Don't fathers know that they may only be revered when they are far away?

—Richard Condon, *A Trembling upon Rome,* 1983

If it were natural for fathers to care for their sons, they would not need so many laws commanding them to do so.

—Phyllis Chesler

The thing to remember about fathers is, they're men.

—Phyllis McGinley, "Girl's-Eye View of Relatives," *Times Three,* 1960

[Fathers] are more trouble than they are worth and likely to abuse children sexually.

— ANON., "Are Fathers Really Necessary?" in *Shrew,* 1973

✿ *Fathers and children never had any natural connection.*

Mothers are a biological necessity; fathers are a social invention.

— MARGARET MEAD

Considering the care and anxiety a woman must have about a child before it comes into the world, it seems to me, by a *natural right,* to belong to her. When men get immersed in the world they seem to lose all sensations, excepting those necessary to continue or produce life! — Are these the privileges of reason! Amongst the feathered race, whilst the hen keeps the young warm, her mate stays by to cheer her; but it is sufficient for a man to condescend to get a child, in order to claim it. — A man is a tyrant!

— MARY WOLLSTONECRAFT, letter to Gilbert Imlay, JANUARY 1, 1794

CANNON FATHER: Male who impregnates explosively and then exits the scene of the female's destruction; one anxious to replace himself without having to participate in his offspring's upbringing.

•

NUCLEAR FAMILY'S NUCLEAR HEAD: Male agitator ruling over a conventional family bombsite; one like to go off/blow off over and over again at the slightest provocation, devastating his own family.

— KATE MUSGRAVE, *Womb with Views,* 1989

⟡ *What was so enthralling, anyway, about the institution called the family?*

Family: A group of closely related persons living under one roof; it is a convenience, often a necessity, sometimes a pleasure, sometimes the reverse; but who first exalted it as an admirable, and almost religious ideal?　　　—ROSE MACAULAY, *The World My Wilderness,* 1950

Family life in America is a minefield, an economic trap for women, a study in disappointment for both sexes.

—ANNE ROIPHE, *Lovingkindness,* 1987

⟡ *Consider the damage family life did to children!*

The potential for emotional maltreatment is directly correlated to the degree the child is dependent upon the adult—the greater the dependence, the greater the potential for abuse.

—PAMPHLET, National Federation for
Child Abuse and Neglect, 1993

The basic rationale for depriving people of rights in a dependency relationship is that certain individuals are incapable or undeserving of the right to take care of themselves and consequently need social institutions specifically designed to safe-guard their position. Along with the family, past and present examples of such arrangements include marriage, slavery, and the Indian reservation system.

—HILLARY RODHAM CLINTON, "Children Under the Law: The
Rights of Children," *Harvard Education Review,* 1973

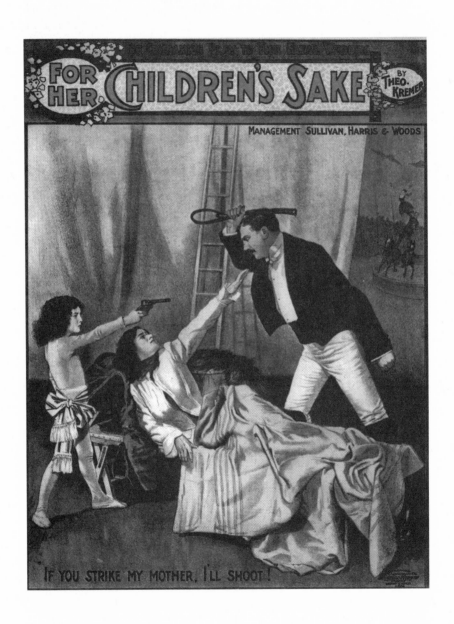

◌ The withering away of the oppressive nuclear family, along with the father, was inevitable in any event, thanks to the all-powerful Welfare State.

Most societies have arranged matters so that a family surrounds and protects mother and child; our families having withered away so that only a male "partner" remains, we find ourselves in a situation where the mother and child(ren) need often to be protected from him rather than by him. Our consensual liaisons grow less durable every year and, if the evidence of wife-battery, rape within marriage and child sexual abuse is to be credited, it is to be hoped that they will soon wither away altogether. The state having taken over the duties of children towards their parents (and allowed the childless among us to face the future without dread) it had better finish the job and take over the duties of the father towards the child.

—GERMAINE GREER, in *Independent Magazine,* MAY 25, 1991

I don't believe that there's enough attention being paid to the fact that we are all lonely children sometimes, and as a government, I think the president probably has to assume that he is adopting a nation of children who need guidance and help and a sense of security and well-being.　　—GOLDIE HAWN, on "Arsenio Hall," AUGUST 1993

◌ The Marquis de Sade predicted that in the ideal republic

Women, having been endowed with considerably more violent penchants for carnal pleasure than we [men], will be able to give themselves over to it wholeheartedly, absolutely free of all encumbering hymeneal ties, of all false notions of modesty. . . .

What, I demand to know, what dangers are there in this license? Children who will lack fathers? Ha! what can that matter in a republic where every individual must have no other dam than the nation, where everyone born is the motherland's child. And how much more they will cherish her, they who, never having known any but her, will comprehend from birth that it is from her alone all must be expected. Do not suppose you are fashioning good republicans so long as children, who ought to belong solely to the republic, remain immured in their families.

— MARQUIS DE SADE, *Philosophy in the Bedroom,* 1795

TAX THEM

•◦• *A potential drawback to the replacement of the family by the omnipotent and omniscient State was the expense of maintaining it. The creative solution, while "men" still possessed any wealth, was to place a special tax on them, especially since they were responsible for the necessity, as well as the expense, of supporting police and the military.*

There are exemptions on the Internal Revenue forms that allow deductions for people over 65 and for people who are blind. An additional exemption on state and federal income-tax forms that allows a deduction for being female would serve two purposes: It would provide gender equity in taxation for crime, and it would so antagonize men as to make them take a second look at their responsibility. . . .

We cannot expect men to police their own. . . . Besides building prisons and increasing incarceration, what is left? Nothing short of

men paying for their own criminal gender. Men must pay for being men.

—June Stephenson, *Men Are Not Cost-Effective*, 1991

❧ *This was only equitable.*

Women spend a tremendous amount of their income protecting themselves from unpleasant situations created by men.... For the most part, women are a calming influence, peacefully beautifying the city ... [but] men can squelch your appreciation for the outdoors by leering, honking and making that monkey-sucking noise if they find a woman attractive.... Cut women a break. Cut us a deal on taxes.

—Lisa Nee, Op-Ed page in *The New York Times*, July 26, 1992

INCARCERATE THEM

❧ *Beyond relieving "men" of their ill-gotten gains, farsighted sapient revolutionaries recognized that "men" must be preemptively imprisoned to prevent them from plying their criminal trade. House arrest was a promising start.*

Progressive universities, such as the University of Utah, initially instituted curfew codes for males. This sensible regulation was also proposed as a national law in the Canadian parliament and elsewhere. A German

M.P. described the advantages of her proposed bill making it illegal for men to be out in public after 10 P.M. in summer and 5 P.M. in winter:

The streets will be much safer for women. . . . [Men] will be able to do more chores around the house. They will be around to help the children with homework and keep their wives company.

With the backing of most of the women voters in this country, I think we can pass this bill. And already we have millions of women on our side.

—THE HON. ANNELORE RESSEL, 1992

CASTRATE THEM

~ *A humane alternative, in keeping with women's kinder and gentler nature, was to relieve the creatures of the burdensome and useless organs that impel them to their characteristic mindless violence.*
Punitive castration has a long and noble history.

In the ancient world, the Egyptians, Persians, Assyrians, Ethiopians, Medes and Hebrews all practiced castration as a means of hu-

miliating their vanquished enemies. So did the Chinese. . . . Anthropologists believe that only among American Indians was it the women . . . who castrated prisoners. Numerous explanations have been offered to account for this exception, but historically it seems that . . . castration of a prisoner was considered a minor bloody chore left to squaws, whereas major tortures that ran on for hours were reserved for the enjoyment of braves. . . .

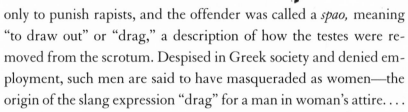

The Egyptians, six thousand years ago, were the first people to punish sex crimes with castration. . . . For first offenders, the ancient Romans crushed a man's gonads between stones. . . . The ancient Greeks used castration only to punish rapists, and the offender was called a *spao,* meaning "to draw out" or "drag," a description of how the testes were removed from the scrotum. Despised in Greek society and denied employment, such men are said to have masqueraded as women—the origin of the slang expression "drag" for a man in woman's attire. . . .

In France, castration as punishment was finally abolished by Napoleon . . . [but] castration as punishment continued in other parts of the world. . . .

—CHARLES PANATI, *Panati's Extraordinary Endings of Practically Everything and Everybody,* 1989

In San Diego, California, between 1955 and 1975, 397 sex offenders chose to be castrated rather than serve a long jail sentence. In Denmark, between 1929 and 1959, 300 prisoners or detainees made the same choice. In Britain, chemical suppressants of the sex urge are preferred. The World Health Organization strongly opposes the whole idea. —REAY TANNAHILL, *Sex in History,* 1980

[With] "chemical castration" . . . the imprisoned rapist is surgically given a subdermal implant of a dime-size disc that contains synthetic female hormones. . . . The time-released treatment is supposedly replacing earlier chemical castration that was done by injection. British articles have reported that a large one-time infusion of female hormones excessively feminized a man, giving him larger breasts and a rounded rump that other male prisoners viewed as irresistible. Such feminized rapists were often themselves raped by inmates, making them victims of their own crime.

—CHARLES PANATI, *Panati's Extraordinary Endings of Practically Everything and Everybody,* 1989

No one can deny the justice of that! But not everyone had the patience to allow the penal system to run its course.

The case of Lorena Bobbitt, who took justice into her own hands and amputated her husband's penis early in 1993, struck a responsive chord in many sapients.

The . . . response of support that comes for Lorena Bobbitt comes from that depth of anger, of feeling there hasn't been adequate resources and recourse and redress of the terrible violence women face.

—PATRICIA IRELAND, president of NOW, on "20/20," 1993

There are a lot of women who . . . wish they'd had a chance to get their own revenge. So I certainly think that explains the number of women who have said, "Yeah, well, he got what he deserved."

—KIM GANDY, executive vice president of NOW, Associated Press report, 1993

Every woman I've talked to about this says, "Way to go!"
—LYNNE M. NELSON, resident of Manassas, Virginia (the Bobbitts'
hometown), in *The New York Times,* NOVEMBER 6, 1993

There are women who say he got what he deserved for being an
insensitive lover alone.
—AMY PAGNOZZI, in the *New York Daily News,* NOVEMBER 10, 1993

He always have orgasm and he doesn't wait for me to have
orgasm. He's selfish. I don't think it's fair, so I pulled back the sheets
and then I did it.   —LORENA BOBBITT, statement to the police
upon her arrest, JUNE 23, 1993

✧ *Mrs. Bobbitt's defense was so successful that a jury naturally acquitted her of any wrongdoing.*
*Medical journals reported an epidemic of genital amputations in
Thailand in the 1970s. Wives who suspected their husbands of infidelity
detached the offending member and tossed it out the door, a practice
known as "feeding the ducks."*

I'd better get home—or the ducks will have something to chew
on.   —THAI SAYING

✧ *This minor surgical procedure appears to have a psychological component. A scholarly inquiry into . . .*

. . . whether witches can with the help of devils really and actually
remove the member, or whether they only do so apparently by some
glamour or illusion. And that they can actually do so is argued *a*

fortiori; for since devils can do greater things than this . . . therefore they can also truly and actually remove men's members. . . .

But when it is performed by witches, it is only a matter of glamour; although it is no illusion in the opinion of the sufferer. For his imagination can really and actually believe that something is not present, since by none of his exterior senses, such as sight or touch, can he perceive that it is present.

From this it may be said that there is a true abstraction of the member in imagination, although not in fact.

—HEINRICH KRAMER AND JOHANN SPRENGER, O.P., *Malleus Maleficarum (Hammer of Witches),* 1486

If you do it psychologically, it's so much more fun.

—FLORENCE KING, on Lorena Bobbitt, 1993

✑ *The hypnagogic solution was part of an ancient tradition, as psychiatrists attest.*

"Castration anxiety" . . . is a very real thing both in folklore and in the [psychiatrist's] office. . . . Outright castration or castration threat, directed by women against men, is amply supported both by clinical and mythological evidence, and in particular the dangerous, devouring vagina is as prominent in myth the world over as it is in

our consulting rooms. . . . But not only the vagina—woman as such is, and is seen as, castrating.

—WOLFGANG LEDERER, M.D., *The Fear of Women,* 1968

[Psychoanalytic] theory has it that the boy fears castration by the father. . . . This is *not* verified by my clinical experience. It is his mother whom he fears. . . . Throughout life, the man fears the woman as castrator, not the man.

—Joseph C. Rheingold, *The Fear of Being a Woman,* 1964

✎ *One wonders why!*

A good part—and definitely the most fun part—of being a feminist is about frightening men. American and Australian feminists have always known this. . . . Of course, there's a lot more to feminism . . . but scaring the shit out of the scumbags is an amusing and necessary part because, sadly, a good many men still respect nothing but strength.   —Julie Burchill, British columnist, in *Time Out,* 1989

We'll wear you [men] like alligator handbags.

—Jane McLoughlin, author of *The Demographic Revolution,* on BBC-TV, "Behind the Headlines," January 9, 1991

✎ *An insight into "the gentler sex":*

We distinguish two sorts of cruelty: that resulting from stupidity . . . [and] the other species of cruelty, fruit of extreme organic sensibility. . . . It is this second kind of cruelty you will most often find in women. . . . Announce a cruel spectacle, a burning, a battle, a combat of gladiators, you will see droves of them come running. . . .

Zingua, Queen of Angola, cruelest of women, killed her lovers as soon as they had had their way with her. . . . Zoé, a Chinese emperor's wife, knew no pleasure equal to what she felt upon witnessing the

execution of criminals; wanting these, she had slaves put to death, and the while would fuck with her husband, and proportioned her discharges to the anguishes she made these wretches endure. . . . Theodora, Justinian's wife, amused herself seeing eunuchs made; and Messalina frigged herself while men were masturbated to death before her. The women of Florida cause their husband's member to swell and they deposit little insects upon the glans, which produces very horrible agonies. . . . When the Spaniards came, [the women] themselves held their husbands while those European barbarians assassinated them. . . . In a word, history furnishes a thousand thousand details of women's cruelty . . . and, thus broadcasting their poison everywhere about, they cause their husbands and their families to despair.

—MARQUIS DE SADE, *Philosophy in the Bedroom,* 1795

 Perhaps Sade was being a bit harsh. Scholars of erotica reported that **men** *enjoy womanly discipline.*

In our scrutiny of [400 years of] flagellant literature, certain patterns begin to emerge. Primarily we find that the most enthusiastic recipients of whipping are men. It becomes further evident that most self-respecting flagellants prefer to have the operation performed on them by women. Since the majority of female flagellators seem to enjoy their work thoroughly, this makes for a very satisfactory arrangement.

—BERNHARDT J. HURWOOD, *The Golden Age of Erotica,* 1965

⟡ This brings us to the subject of recreational castration. Historians believe that Sammu-ramat, a 9th-century B.C. Queen of Assyria who reigned for 42 years, was its first practitioner. Described by Diodorus the Sicilian (1st century B.C.) as "half goddess and half queen, great general, great engineer and great statesman," she provided the basis for the Greek legend of Semiramis. Herodotus called her "the most beautiful, most cruel, most powerful and most lustful of Oriental queens."

There are conflicting accounts as to why she became such an enthusiastic castrator. According to one source she had men so mutilated in order to prevent opposition to her female rule. Others assert that she was motivated by jealousy. After spending the night in the arms of the handsomest man in the army, it was said the queen would

have him castrated to prevent him from giving the same pleasure to any other woman.

—BERNHARDT J. HURWOOD,
*The Golden Age
of Erotica,* 1965

⟡ A delightful apotheosis is achieved when the creatures are persuaded to perform the operation on themselves.

The Greek historian Herodotus tells of a unique

treatment of a rapist or adulterer devised by the Samaritans, fifth-century B.C. nomads. A sturdy rope would be drawn tightly around the man's genitals, then he would be hanged from a tree, one hand bound behind his back, a sharp knife placed in his other hand. If he chose, he could free himself by self-castration.

—CHARLES PANATI, *Panati's Extraordinary Endings of Practically Everything and Everybody,* 1989

⟡ *In certain sophisticated societies, the practice of self-castration had a religious component.*

The most dramatic feature of the [Hybristika] cult was the voluntary self-castration of male devotees; their severed genitals in their hands, the worshipers ran through the streets and threw them into some house, in return for woman's clothing which they wore from then on. Or else the genitalia were carried in solemn procession in baskets on the heads of priestesses, taken to the innermost shrine . . . washed, anointed, sometimes even gilded, and then buried.

—WOLFGANG LEDERER, M.D., *The Fear of Women,* 1968

[In Rome] the novitiate priests of Cybele ceremonially castrated themselves on the *dies sanguinis,* the "day of blood." Latin sources are not explicit about the ceremony, but it seems probable that it followed the lines laid down in Syria when, to the insistent sound of music and chanting, priests and novitiates cut and slashed themselves, dervish-like, before the temple. Then, when religious excitement was at its most frenzied, the novitiate flung off his clothes, grasped the ceremonial sword, and with a single blow castrated himself. . . .

What the eunuch did with the family jewels—"the precious," as the Chinese called them—offers an interesting sidelight. . . . The Syrian worshippers of Cybele . . . genitals in hand, ran through the streets until they could run no more, and then sent them flying through the nearest householder's window. . . . In Rome Cybele's priests, more sedately, buried "the precious" in the ground. . . . The Chinese eunuch . . . [kept] them "in common pint measures hermetically closed, and placed on a high shelf," so that they might, when the time came, be buried with their owner in his coffin.

—REAY TANNAHILL, *Sex in History,* 1980

❧ *Even the patriarchy's late second millennium provided plentiful career opportunities for eunuchs. Singing castrati, popular in Europe for over 1,700 years, persisted in the Vatican chorus until 1922. In the Middle East the operation continued to be performed well into the 20th century to produce harem guards and docile slaves. The last imperial Chinese palace eunuch died in 1951, the same year George Jorgensen, an American ex-GI, became Christine Jorgensen, the first modern surgical transsexual. Thus one era ended as another began.*

Unfortunately, some men resisted this friendly solution.

KILL THEM

❧ *Considering this deplorable lack of cooperation, as well as the vile nature of the male beast, one wonders why more pre-Revolutionary sapients didn't invoke the ultimate solution.*

Of course, many did.

I never sees men or dogs but what I aches to kill them.

—AUGUSTA MAIN, arrested for murder, 1897

My attitude toward men who mess around is simple: If you find 'em, kill 'em.

— LORETTA LYNN

April 24, 1774. A woman was committed . . . for the murder of a man with whom she had cohabited for nineteen years, and had bore him eleven children. She cut his throat in a fit of jealousy, and that not putting an immediate end to his life she dashed out his brains with a poker. Her resentment was so strong, and she was so far from denying the fact, on her examination, that she owned, if the deed could be recalled, she would again repeat it.

— ANON., *Gentleman's Magazine,*
1774

I shot him 'cause I love him, God damn him!

— TESSIE WALL
(Murderous Madam from California), 19TH CENTURY

There will be a time you bury me
Or I bury you in the garden.

— TOMIOKA TAEKO, "Living Together," 1935

My mother buried three husbands, and two of them were just napping.
—RITA RUDNER

∾ *This was obviously a recurrent dream.*

The comfortable estate of widowhood is the only hope that keeps up a wife's spirits.
—JOHN GAY, *The Beggar's Opera,* 1728

Perhaps men should think twice before making widowhood our only path to power.
—GLORIA STEINEM

When you consider what a chance women have to poison their husbands, it's a wonder there isn't more of it done.
—KIN HUBBARD

∾ *H. L. Mencken on "The Wife's Revenge":*

A woman, if she hates her husband (and many of them do), can make life so sour and obnoxious to him that even death upon the gallows seems sweet by comparison. This hatred, of course, is often, and perhaps almost invariably, quite justified. To be the wife of an ordinary man, indeed, is an experience that must be very hard to bear. The hollowness and vanity of the fellow, his petty meanness and stupidity, his puling sentimentality and credulity, his bombastic air of a

cock on a dunghill, his anaesthesia to all whispers and summonings of the spirit, above all, his loathsome clumsiness in amour—all these things must revolt any woman above the lowest. To be the object of the oafish affections of such a creature . . . cannot be expected to give any genuine joy to a woman of sense and refinement. . . . But there must be innumerable revolts in secret, even so, and one sometimes wonders that so few women, with the thing so facile and so safe, poison their husbands. Perhaps it is not quite as rare as vital statistics make it out; the death rate among husbands is very much higher than among wives. More than once, indeed, I have gone to the funeral of an acquaintance who died suddenly, and observed a curious glitter in the eyes of the inconsolable widow.

—H. L. MENCKEN, *In Defense of Women,*
Part IV, "The Wife's Revenge," 1922

᛫᠊᛫ *Clearly the world was bound to be a more amenable place for the delicate sex once the evil predators were neutralized.*

I thought their tongues should have been fine-sliced and their hearts hacked to pieces—those men whose perverted minds and inconceivable hostility fueled by vulgar envy so flamed that they deny, stupidly ranting, that women are able to attain eloquence . . . those pathetic men, doomed to rascality, whose patent insanity I lash with unleashed tongue. —LAURA CERETA, 1487

Dead men tell no lies.

—BARBIE LIBERATION ORGANIZATION (switched voice boxes on Barbie and G.I. Joe dolls, Christmas, 1993)

Dead Men Don't Rape!

•

The way to a man's heart is through his chest.

•

So many men . . . So little ammunition!

—FEMINIST SLOGANS, 1993

I don't have the time every day to put on makeup. I need that time to clean my rifle. —HENRIETTE MANTEL, 1992

How can a revolution be made without executions?

—V. I. LENIN (1870–1924)

Every society rests on the death of men.
> —OLIVER WENDELL HOLMES, JR. (1841–1935)

It seldom happens, I think, that a man has the civility to die when all the world wishes it.
> —MARIE DE SÉVIGNÉ, letter to her daughter, MARCH 1, 1680

I used to lie in bed beside my husband after those fights and wish I had the courage to bash in his head with a frying pan.
> —SALLY KEMPTON, "Cutting Loose," in *Esquire,* JULY 1970

᠆᠊ *By the late 1990s, androcide had been legalized in all but the most backward societies.*

Twelve distinct female-only defenses allow a woman who commits a premeditated murder to have the charges dropped or significantly reduced. No man has successfully used any of these defenses in similar circumstances. Nor do men have any equivalent "male only" defenses. . . . Taken together, the twelve female-only defenses allow almost any woman to take it upon herself to exercise the death penalty. . . .

By the 1990s, states such as California and Ohio allowed a woman to kill her sleeping husband and claim self-defense because she "*felt* helpless." . . . For the first time in American history, premeditated murder . . . was called self-defense—but only if a woman was accused; and only if a man was murdered. . . .

Ohio became the fifteenth state to allow women to murder their sleeping husbands and possibly get away with the murder by

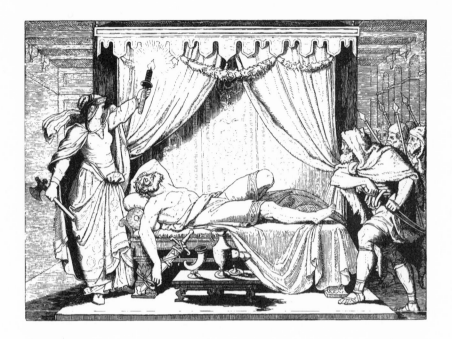

claiming past abuse (their husbands were not in a position to argue the claim). They were not required to prove they were in imminent danger of being killed without any possible *physical* escape. On this basis, the governor of Ohio released from prison "The Ohio Twenty-five." . . .

The government is not allowed to kill someone first and declare him or her an abuser later—only a woman can do that to a man.

—WARREN FARRELL, *The Myth of Male Power,* 1993

Woman Who Shot Mate 5 Times Gets Probation.

—MARY BALOUSEK, article headline,
Wisconsin State Journal, AUGUST 19, 1988

Women don't kill men unless they've been pushed to a point of desperation.

— LENORE WALKER, defense attorney, in Isabel Wilkerson,
"Clemency Granted to 25 Women Convicted for Assault
or Murder," *The New York Times,* DECEMBER 22, 1990

THE SELF-NEUTRALIZING MALE

‹◦› *It would have been far more humane and easier all around if the savages had had either the ability to transform or the decency to eliminate themselves.*
A moderate view:

Some people say that men are naturally, or biologically, aggressive. But this leaves us at an impasse. If the values of society are power-oriented, there is no chance that men would agree to be medicated into an humane state.

The other alternative that has been suggested is to eliminate men as biologically incapable of humane relationships and therefore a menace to society. . . . But the proposal to eliminate men . . . assumes that men constitute a kind of social disease, and that by "men" is meant those individuals with certain typical genital characteristics . . . [that] are held to determine the organism in every biological respect thus determining the psychic structure as well. It may be that as in other mental derangements, and I do believe that men behave in a mentally deranged manner toward women, there is a biochemical correspondence, but this would be ultimately behaviorally determined, not genetically.

I believe that the sex roles—both male and female—must be destroyed, not the individuals who happen to possess either a penis or a vagina, or both, or neither. . . . Men must, at the very least, cooperate in curing themselves. . . . It is superhuman, but the only alternative— the elimination of males as a biological group—is subhuman.

—TI-GRACE ATKINSON, "Radical Feminism," c. 1970

ᐧᐁᐧ *Not all visionaries were so forbearing.*

GIVE HIM LIBERTIES OR GIVE HIM DEATH!: Rousing feminist cry in behalf of the man who loudly swears he couldn't live without sex, i.e., intercourse, yet who lacks the courage to kill himself when inevitably necessary.   —KATE MUSGRAVE, *Womb with Views,* 1989

Give him enough rope and he will hang himself.

—CHARLOTTE BRONTË, *Shirley,* 1849

ᐧᐁᐧ *A rousing battle cry from the artist Valerie Solanis, founder of the Society for Cutting Up Men (S.C.U.M.), also known as the would-be assassin of Andy Warhol:*

Life in this society being, at best, an utter bore and no aspect of society being at all relevant to women, there remains to civic-minded, responsible, thrill-seeking females only to overthrow the government, eliminate the money system, institute complete automation, and destroy the male sex.

It is now technically possible to reproduce without the aid of males . . . and to produce only females. We must begin immediately to do so. . . .

The male, because of his obsession to compensate for not being female combined with his inability to relate and to feel compassion, has made of the world a shitpile. He is responsible for: War . . . Money, Marriage and Prostitution . . . Fatherhood and Mental Illness . . . Authority and Government . . . Prejudice . . . Ugliness . . . Hate and Violence . . . Disease and Death. . . .

SCUM will kill all men who are not in the Men's Auxiliary of SCUM. Men in the Men's Auxiliary are those men who are working diligently to eliminate themselves. . . .

The sick, irrational men, those who attempt to defend themselves against their disgustingness, when they see SCUM barreling down on them, will cling in Terror to Big Mama with her Big Bouncy Boobies, but Boobies won't protect them against SCUM. . . . Men who are rational, however, won't kick or struggle or raise a distressing fuss, but will just sit back, relax, enjoy the show, and ride the waves to their demise.

—VALERIE SOLANIS, *The S.C.U.M. Manifesto,* 1967

DEAD MEN DON'T JOKE

 ◌ *Some traditional parables:*

A young woman visits a fortuneteller. The Gypsy peers into the crystal ball, and then announces in a loud voice, "Prepare for tragedy: Your husband is about to die a violent death!"

After a moment of silence the young woman squints at the crystal ball and asks, "Will I be acquitted?"

•

A woman goes into a sporting-goods store to buy a rifle. "It's for my husband," she tells the clerk.

"Did he tell you what gauge to get?" the clerk asks.

"Don't be silly," she says. "He doesn't even know I'm going to shoot him!"

•

"I just buried my second husband and I vowed never to marry again," said the woman to her new friend. "That's a shame," said the friend. "What happened to your husbands?" "Well, the first one died from eating poison mushrooms, and the second one was shot to death." "Shot to death!" said her friend. "That's horrible! How did it happen?" The widow shrugged. "He wouldn't eat the mushrooms."

•

"Remember," the doctor told the elderly couple, "no physical exertion for the mister. And that includes sex. It could kill him." That night, to avoid temptation, the old man slept downstairs on the couch. But at 3 A.M. he woke up horny and started for the bedroom. Halfway up, he met his wife. "Oh, honey," he said, "I was just coming up the stairs to die." "And I," she replied, "was just coming downstairs to kill you."

•

After her husband passed away, the mortuary called the widow and said that there was some confusion as to whether he was to be buried or cremated.

"Let's not take any chances," she said, "Do both."

•

Why did the woman insist on burying her husband twelve feet under?

Because deep down, he was a good person.

•

"Mommy, Mommy, Daddy's getting up!"
   "Shut up and reload."

•

"Mommy, Mommy, why is Daddy so pale?"
   "Shut up and keep digging."

•

How do you stop your husband from drowning?
   Take your foot off his head.

•

How do you get your man out of a tree?
   Cut the rope.

—U.S., British, Canadian and Australian jokes, 1985–1993

∽ *Now that "men" have been successfully subdued and restricted to their cozy and luxurious all-male colonies, such jests have become obsolete—along with such benighted social constructs as "men" themselves; the set of oppressive and disgusting practices that used to be known as "sex"; the legalized theft that used to be called "private property"; the environmental rapes once dignified with the titles "technology" and "science"; and a host of lesser evils, such as the antidemocratic practice of "joking."*

The occasional senti(person)talist can still be heard expressing sympathy and even a wistful sort of affection for the obsolete beasts. Some few sapients have even been heard to grumble from time to time about how cold it gets around the fire at night. But these antisocial habits too will die, now that the murderous patriarchal conceits known as "disagreement," "opposition," "conflict" and "controversy" have been ruthlessly banned. With the cleansing of the libraries that is now under way, soon even the memory of "men" will fade, except for chronicles such as this of their treachery, violence and inhumanity.

•

More tears are shed over answered prayers than over unanswered prayers.

—St. Theresa of Avila

ACKNOWLEDGMENTS

This book was produced with the help of the following sapients and near-sapients, to whom the author is gratefully indebted: Alane Mason, enlightened editor; Lori Andreozzi, relentless researcher; Britt-Alexis Russ, tireless typist; Lynn Chu and Glen Hartley, affirmative agents; Charles Portney, supportive partner (who patiently endured the retelling of countless stupid-men jokes); Jonathan Starr, best brother and business partner; and Roberta Rosenthal, artist and picture researcher, whose efforts made this project glow.

Additional thanks to: Diane Covan, Esq.; Professor Neil Gilbert of U.C., Berkeley; Mary Gums of Daktronics, South Dakota; journalist Ed Hayman; computer consultant Martha Lambert; Sufi Richardson of Kalepa Farm, Maui; Professor Christina Hoff Sommers of Clark University, Worcester, Massachusetts; folic person Lita Starr; editorial assistant Celia Wren; and social commentator Cathy Young—all of whom kindly contributed extra stupid-men jokes, extra wise insights, or both.

Special thanks to the New York Public Library Picture Collection, Dover Publications, Inc., and Roz Warren.

TEXT CREDITS

Selections from *Lysistrata* by Aristophanes, translated by Douglass Parker, translation copyright ©1964 by William Arrowsmith, used by permission of Dutton Signet, a division of Penguin Books USA Inc. Selections from *Medea and Other Plays* by Euripides, translated by Philip Vellacott, translation copyright ©1963 by Philip Vellacott, reproduced by permission of Penguin Books Ltd. "Annul in Me My Manhood" by Brother Antoninu O. P., copyright ©1957 by University of Detroit Press. "The Couch Potato" copyright ©1992 by Vesle Fenstermaker, used by permission of Vesle Fenstermaker, excerpted from *Women's Glibbers,* ed. by Roz Warren. "A Woman Tells Men" copyright ©1987 by Shary Flenniken, used by permission of Shary Flenniken.

INDEX OF SOURCES